*An air of the dream clings to the place, a dream rising out of reality.*

—ARTHUR MILLER, *Death of a Salesman*

# LIVING ON A DREAM

## A MARRIAGE TALE

### PATT BLUE

*University Press of Mississippi / Jackson*

TO MY MOTHER AND TO MY HUSBAND, LARRY

The names of all the people and many of the places in this book have been changed. The main text is oral history as told to me by my mother, called here Willie Louise Davis Clarkson. My own narrative is set in a different typeface. Most of the photographs were made by my father, given the name J.W. Clarkson, Jr.; some were made by Louise as she grabbed the camera or took her turn. The pictures I took as a child and later as a photographer are on the cover and on pages 1, 5, 16, 62, 78-79, 145, 154-155, 156, 160, 183, 190-191, 230-231, and 233. Others were made by unknown photographers. Photograph on pages 14-15 is courtesy Market House Museum, Paducah, Kentucky.

Copyright © 1998 by Patt Blue
All rights reserved
Designed by John A. Langston
Manufactured in Canada
CIP data appear on page 240

# PREFACE

*I was twenty–two, pregnant, unmarried, and living at the Washington Square Home for unwed mothers in New York City. The father of my baby was a French artist I had met in New Orleans, twenty years older than I. He laughed when I told him the news. He said that it was probably just something I was imagining so that I could write about it. Six months later, I watched a social worker walk towards the hospital door carrying a baby wrapped in pink bunting. I had just given birth, and I named the baby Sonya, after a Dostoyevsky character who, like my mother, was selfless, compassionate, and faithful. When the door opened, I knew that, in a moment, Sonya would be gone forever, but no words came forth as I watched her disappear. I still have the picture of her taken when she was one hour old; it's in a pink paper frame that says "Well, here I am."*

*Five years later I woke up to the smells of another hospital. "You were brought in around midnight—you're a lucky girl!" the nurse said. Looking into the sunlight, I remembered being eleven, back in Kentucky, with the smell of green grass coming in through the open doors and windows. I saw myself happily awaken, jump up, throw on any old thing, and run outside into the yard, talking to my dog, Skipper, and to all the trees and flowers around me. The mimosas were in bloom and the magnolia leaves were shiny—in the quiet I felt embraced by love and friendship. I was glad to be alive. I had somehow been spared from suicide, but I had little memory of why I had gulped down all those black pills. My boyfriend had a way of gazing off into the distance when I was talking to him. He loved women, especially my roommates. When he came over, he would hug my roommate first, explaining that he didn't want her to feel left out. His behavior cut into an unhealed wound that would take a lifetime to scar over—my father's habit of flirting and womanizing. My release from the hospital depended on care from an assigned psychologist who began immediately asking about my family.*

*My parents, J.W. and Louise, were married to each other, and then divorced, three times. By the time I was eighteen we had lived in eleven houses, having moved from our hometown in western Kentucky down to New Orleans and finally to south Texas. As a child I adored my father, who was charming and clever. We laughed and played together; he taught me things and was amused by my antics. Then he changed, and our family became a ruin. My mother was kind and loving and wanted to believe his repeated promises, so she held firm to her beliefs. We were always leaving, hoping to start a new life, running from J.W.'s girlfriend, Norma, and her threats. My two brothers, Wiley and Davy, and I were in the path of our parents' self–destruction.*

*For a long time I denied that there had been any damage. It was photography that finally made me look at myself and begin to see the truth of my upbringing. My introduction to photography had begun when I was a child watching my father hold a print up in the amber light of his darkroom, a tiny room in our house on Clover Street in Greenfield, Kentucky. He was an amateur photographer, and, no matter where we lived, even if it meant that my brother had to sleep in the living room, there was always a darkroom. Later, when I began taking pictures, like him, I photographed people. He photographed his wife and children. I photographed strangers in pain. I haven't seen my father for thirty years, but we will be forever linked by photography. When I stand looking down into the ground glass, I am stabbed and embraced by the memory of a father whose example I have followed.*

*I have been drawn to photograph what I most feared and wanted to understand: unwed mothers abandoning their infants, a poor family trying to survive, people bound to their wheelchairs and beds. I once photographed and directed strange, naked men while they acted out inner torment. In one, a man held a gun to his head for hours in my studio of black walls and hot scorching lights. In my work I have identified with struggle and with suffering, and in my dreams I have fought demons, women that meta-*

*morphosed into men, drooling giants, and slovenly washerwomen — mother and father, my therapist insisted. My past has driven my work in ways that I am only now fully recognizing.*

*One morning when visiting my mother, I asked her to pose nude for me. She exclaimed in her southern twang, "My gawd, Patricia, I cannot believe how much you are just like your father!" and, opening her closet door, she pointed to a battered tan briefcase leaning against a carton overflowing with letters, negatives, photographs, journals, and reams of curling, yellowed papers. Some dog-eared eight-by-ten black-and-white pinups made by my father in the 1950s were pulled out. I was especially struck by one, an image of my mother kneeling on a tiny towel and wearing nothing but her high heels, a child's crayon lying nearby on the floor. The nude I had made of her was a cold, steady, formal arrangement. My father's photograph was much better, I thought, honest and purely drawn, capturing his wife's pain as he forced her to sit and sit until the image suited him.*

*I had grown up with many of J.W.'s photographs displayed on my parents' dresser or under the glass of our coffee table, but now, looking at them with a photographer's eye, I had an epiphany of sorts. I realized how cynical I had become about documentary photographers like myself who knew how to make a picture, a gorgeous one, even of someone dying. My father's photographs, which mirrored his emotions and his need both to control and to preserve his family on film, touched me deeply. I felt that my style had become somewhat tainted by my knowledge and professional practice, and I was inspired by the freshness I observed in his images. They are carefully posed portraits, not the typically candid birthday, graduation, and holiday pictures found in most family albums. Though we have always thought of his photographs as our family pictures, I don't believe he made them with the family album in mind. J.W. was obsessed with a need to be in charge, so the idea of controlling the ephemeral existence of his wife, children, and girlfriends must have generated in him much excitement and enthusiasm for photography. I think of his pictures both as a way to look into his mind and as testimony to his wish to fix reality by directing, framing, collecting, and making evidence visible.*

*Over a period of ten years I have traveled to our many family homes, photographing, retrieving memories, and writing down my thoughts. My mother handed over to me all the family photographs and negatives. I have copied, enlarged, lightened, darkened, cropped, and sequenced them with the utmost respect and sincerity. My manipulations have been an effort not to alter J.W.'s photographs but to distill their essence. I made three long trips to Houston to interview my mother. Her stories are the heart of this document. My father's presence was strongly felt; with his photographs spread around us, we hacked our way back through the thicket of the past.*

*Our differences became evident as we went—I revealed my resentment that she wasn't the mother I had wanted, the one who was a fighter against her husband's dominance, and she put up defenses to my questioning and criticism. We battled. Occasionally Louise forgot that it was her daughter asking the questions and told me more than she meant to. There were times when she repeated a story but gave it a different slant. We were often in disagreement and also often in each other's arms, trying to understand and to heal our lives by the telling of this story.*

# LIVING ON A DREAM

THE OHIO RIVER VALLEY FLOOD OF 1937

LOUISE WITH HER FATHER'S FRAMED RIVERBOAT MASTER AND PILOT'S LICENSE, 1975

# 1

## MAMA CAN'T WEAR RED

# FIRST INTERVIEW
*June 10, 1987*

*It was still dark at 5 A.M. when the Sunset Limited arrived in Houston from New Orleans, where I had been for a month photographing and writing. Loaded down with camera bags, I made my exit and called a cab from a pay phone. As I got closer to my mother's house on West Hosanna, I felt fearful of what lay ahead. Hot air rushed in through the open windows as I rode down a ghostly San Pablo Avenue, past the bus stop where Louise waited in the boiling south Texas sun each day for the bus that carried her to Mrs. Jannaway's mansion. My mother had worked there for a decade as a companion to the elderly woman. When she was laid off, she still visited and worried over her former employer, even though she had worked for years for a dollar an hour and without benefits of any kind. What my mother called kindness bothered my sense of propriety. The driver stopped in front of a small, pale green duplex. I knew the house and hated the failure it represented. The porch light burned expectantly. Weeping into my chest, my mother greeted me, her daughter and rescuer. Her embrace was one of relief that she would now be less alone with her memories. I felt as tall as a giant and rail thin against her small, warm, fleshy body. I put my arm around her and we walked towards the house where we would spend the next week talking about the past.*

# TEARS IN HIS EYES

The first time I met my husband-to-be I was on my front porch at Seventeenth and Clover Street in Greenfield [Kentucky], barefooted, sitting up on a swing. This was our new house after the flood and I didn't know anyone in the neighborhood. This great big tall boy came up and introduced himself as J.W. Clarkson, Jr. He was real friendly. He said he lived across the street. At that time I was about sixteen years old.

Your father and I were just friends. He liked to dance and I liked to dance, so on Friday and Saturday nights we'd go out to what they used to call back in those days roadhouses. Mama let me go out with J.W. 'cause he talked real nice and had manners — she knew his daddy before I was born. J.W. had that attitude like, you know, he knew it all. He was so smart in his books that he didn't have to devote much time to studying. I know he said they put him ahead a couple of grades. At that time he was getting ready to graduate.

I had to quit school in the eighth grade. Mama had a nervous breakdown and I had to drop out to take care of her. Your grandmother stayed in bed all the time when I was a little girl, she was always sick. She had put me in this Seventh-Day Adventist School, 'cause that's what Mama was — and I mean a strict Seventh-Day Adventist! When I went back to school I didn't feel right — I think that's what made me want to quit. I felt different than the other kids. I tried to register at another school but their studies was just too hard for what I'd been learning and they wanted to put me back. I didn't want to go back, I was too embarrassed — I felt stupid.

After graduating, J.W. had gone to live in Cincinnati and he was going to the university there trying to study to be a lawyer. But he said he couldn't pay what it cost — this was the depression, and so he got a pretty good job working as an insurance man in his uncle's company there in Cincinnati. I got me a job in the hosiery mill — I turned and boxed stockings on the night shift. I don't know why but my mother let me go down there and get a job. I sure regret quitting school. I will regret it all my life.

The night your father asked me to marry him it was close to Christmas in 1937. J.W. asked me would I go to a New Year's Eve dance with him. I told him I would. He was kind of flirty a little bit and he acted like he liked me, but I couldn't hardly believe it — I always thought J.W. was too old for me. He seemed like he was much older than the rest of the boys. I think it must have been the way he dressed. He wore a blue serge suit with a white shirt, French cuffs and stuff like that. I know all my friends would say, "My goodness, Louise, he's too old for you!"

I went with J.W. to that New Year's dance at the Irvin Cobb Hotel and they had a roof garden up there and a good band. I remember when the intermission came and we had to go downstairs, this boy I knew walked up to me and the music was playing out of the hotel and he grabbed me on the sidewalk and started dancing with me. Well, J.W. just walked over to that boy and took his hand off of me and said, "She's with me!" At that time I was nineteen years old. We went on back in and for some reason J.W. started telling me how much he liked me. He said, "I think I like you enough that I'd like to marry you." I laughed it off 'cause I liked J.W., but I was still young and I felt like I wasn't ready to settle down. I always thought that if you married you couldn't be playing around. I thought J.W. was too fast for me. I wasn't for sure about him — I had this feeling inside of me... I remember this girl I worked with at the hosiery mill — she was older — one night we got off work and she said, "Come on, Louise, my boyfriend will drive us home." Well, it was J.W. that picked us up and he was real late, like about an hour late! God, did she bawl him out! Come to find out later that J. W. was with another girl and they went out of town and he couldn't make it back on time. He treated this girl I worked with something terrible! I could tell he didn't care anything about her.

That night at the Cobb Hotel he kept on saying, "You know, I believe that I want to marry you—do you love me?"

"I think a lot of you, but we don't know each other long enough to really be talking this serious."

He said, "I been knowing you for a long time and I been thinking about you a long time and I don't think that I know anybody that I would like to marry like I would you."

I really was shocked!

"Are you going to give me an answer?"

"Well, this is kind of surprising for you to talk like this to me."

"Maybe for you but it's not for me. I'm really serious."

Well, I tried to throw it off. I didn't want to talk about it because I didn't feel serious. But anyway, we went on dancing and having a good time—when he brought me home it was about four o'clock in the morning. He kissed me on the corner by my house and told me that he loved me. He looked me straight in the eyes and said, "If you don't want to marry me, I'll leave and go back to Cincinnati and you'll never see me again." I went in the house and thought I would just try to ignore it...I couldn't believe he was serious...I just thought he had been drinking and was just blowing off. The next morning Mama came and woke me up and told me J. W. was here. I jumped up real fast thinking, "Oh, what am I going to tell him!" I walked into the kitchen and J. W. was leaning up against the cabinet and he had his head hanging down. When I walked in there he just kind of walked over and grabbed my hand and pulled me over close to him. "Have you been thinking about what I told you?" I looked up at

him and I said, "You really mean this . . . what you said last night, you still mean it?"

"Yes, I want an answer!"

I was about ready to say, "I'm sorry, I cannot get married. I'm not ready," and I looked up at him and he looked so sad and I felt so sorry for him. He said, "I promise you I'll be real good to you—I'll give you everything that you always wanted—all the things your

J.W.'S FIRST CAR, C. 1936

mother makes you do you'll never have to do again." He just kept going on ... I wanted to say, "No, I can't marry you," and when I looked up at him I saw tears in his eyes. I felt so bad ... and he kept staring at me and all at once, to tell you the truth, I didn't have the will power to tell him that I would not marry him, so I said, "Yes, okay, I'll marry you."

He was so happy, he picked me up in the air and whizzed me

around and he would put me down and pick me up again! He was crazy, absolutely crazy—he couldn't believe that I said I would marry him!

Your daddy and I got married in the springtime. One Saturday we were sitting out in the car and he was kissing and necking and all that because your father was a very, very affectionate man. All at once he wanted to go get married. He said, "Why can't we just go and get married today?"

I said, "Oh no, not today, maybe we better wait for a while."

"What's the use of waiting, we're going to have to go do it anyway?"

"That's true, but where are we going to stay?"

"Let's not worry about that—we can go to my father's house."

"My mother will have a fit!"

"Yes, but don't worry about that. After we get married things will be different."

So we went down to the corner and around the corner to find our friends, Doris and George. They thought it was funny. They said yes, they would go, so they jumped in the car and we were laughing and talking and going down the road headed for Benton, Kentucky. J.W. was very excited. I tried not to think about what was gonna happen to me. He kept driving down the highway with one hand and I said, "You keep both hands on the wheel!" He kept on saying, "Oh, don't worry about it—lay your head over here on my shoulder." We went on laughing and singing, going towards Benton. I felt kind of scared. I thought, "Oh, my gosh, what are we going to do? Where are we going to stay?" I was thinking about all kinds of things! J.W. just said, "Don't worry about nothing, I'll protect you!"

We got to Benton and went into the courthouse and we flew up the steps and ran down the hall. J.W. said, "My girl and I want to get married...!" This man there looked at me and looked at the other guy and winked. He said to me, "How old are you?" I said, "I'm nineteen." He asked J.W. how old he was and he said he was twenty-two. Then this man said, "Well, all right, if you all want to get married, I guess you're old enough to know what you're doing." He got everything ready and started performing the marriage vows and everything. I had hold of J.W.'s hand during the ceremony—I remember my hand was sweaty and his hand felt cold. The man filled out some papers and J.W. signed them and I signed them, then he says, "Well, now you're married, good luck to you." J.W. grabbed me around the waist and squeezed me and then we flew down the hall and got in the car. We went straight on back to Greenfield.

# A WRINKLED BEDSPREAD

I never had a father around the house when I was growing up. My daddy was a riverboat captain—he was always on the river. Poppa could be gone for three or four months at a time and when he got home from his travels, all the neighborhood kids would sit on our front porch listening to his tales. He'd bring in his grip one day and Mama would put fresh clothes back in that grip and somebody'd call up and say, "Captain Louis, we have a run for you, can you come down here in the morning?" When I was a little girl, Mama and I would go with Poppa. One time I even had my Christmas on the Mississippi River.

Mama was the boss. When I was little, all Mama did was fuss and raise hell around the house all the time. I was afraid of her. My father was, too. My daddy didn't even drive a car—Mama drove. She would not let my daddy handle his own money. He wanted to do everything to please my mother, just like a child he'd give all his money up to her. I loved my daddy and he loved me. My poor daddy—one day he fell out of the pilothouse, the chair give way with him and he fell backwards down the little steps. His head was turned to the side. Can you imagine somebody going straight and looking sideways, that was my daddy. He had to sleep sitting up in a chair next to Mama's bed.

Mama carried on something terrible after she found out J. W. and I got married. She liked to fell in the middle of the floor. She was sobbing and screaming. "You should have talked to me about it! You all are gonna be sorry the way you all have treated me. Oh, my God, what am I going to do! I've lost my girl!" Mama was carrying on so much J. W. and I promised that we would stay with her in her house for one year. Well, we stayed three years 'cause she acted like a little pampered child. She said, "You all can't go off and leave me, I'll be all by myself." So, we fixed up our own little apartment upstairs in Mama's house. Of course, everything was Mama's. She wanted me to be her housekeeper and she wanted J. W. to be her chauffeur. That's how she treated us.

I remember one time Mama came in late one afternoon and I had my little apartment all cleaned up, I had supper started and I was waiting for J. W. to come in from work. I had one of these kind of silk pearly bedspreads on my bed. It was only for looks, you couldn't be sitting on it or laying on it. Mama came in and just laid her body clear across the bed. I said, "Mama, please get up off the bed. The bedspread was so nice and smooth and clean, you lay on it and you're gonna get it all wrinkly! She looked up at me and she said, "This bed is mine and this bedspread's mine." I said, "Yes, I know it is." I felt kind of hurt so when J. W. came in that evening, I told him, "I don't care where we go, but I want to get out of this house, I've stayed here long enough."

# A STRANGE MAN

People called your granddaddy "Old Man Clarkson," because when
Jackie Lee, J. W.'s mother, married him she was only fifteen years old.
He was twice her age. They said she was so young she had to take the
ribbons out of her hair for the preacher to let her marry. Jackie Lee
was a very beautiful woman and Old Man Clarkson was very jealous
of her. When your daddy was twelve years old, his mother ran away
and left him and his two brothers—Jamie was eight and Dewey was
still in diapers. She never came back. The daddy raised the boys.

I remember I thought my father-in-law was a very strange man. I
know he made a good business out of that piano store he owned in
Greenfield. He wasn't poor but he lived poor, he was just stingy. He
was so tight he wouldn't even turn on the lights and gas in his house.
His son Jamie had to get a job working in a Jew store downtown selling clothes to get lights turned on in the house. J. W. and his father
never did get along too well. J. W. was always afraid of his father. His
father was mean, I thought. One time I talked to him and I said,
"You know, it's a shame way back that you and Jackie Lee couldn't
have made it." And he says, "I don't want to talk about it!" He said,
"Just because a woman has a baby that don't mean nothing. Any old
cat or dog can give birth."

I remember the first time I met my mother-in-law, I looked up
and I saw this woman standing at my door . . . I thought, "Who in the
world is this well-to-do woman at my door?" She was dressed in a
navy blue suit and had a beautiful red hat on her head—but the
thing about it was, Dewey must have been on the porch or something—he must have been about fifteen years old—and I heard
this woman say, "Dewey, do you know who this is?" I heard him
say, "No, I don't think I know who you are." She said, "This is your

mother." Then I thought, "Oh my God, this is Jackie Lee!" She peeped through the screen door and Mr. Clarkson was sitting there in the front room. She said, "I'm Jackie Lee," and Old Man Clarkson said, "Yeah, I know." Just as independent as a hog on ice! — but your grandmother never showed her feelings — never let on how she truly felt — no, she was always smiling and she always dressed and looked beautiful.

Your daddy was your grandmother's favorite. She told me she always felt closer to him than she did to Jamie or Dewey. After she disappeared, your father didn't see his mother again until he was grown up — must have been about eighteen or nineteen years old — I know he was out of high school. He went down to where his mother lived in Louisiana and he got a job working on the roads or something like that and he hadn't been there very long before he took appendicitis. I know Jackie Lee told me that J. W. was real bad off sick and gangrene set up inside of him. When she thought he was gonna die, she said she had to get in touch with Old Man Clarkson 'cause she was having a hard time back in those days. She said she had to borrow money to catch a bus to go to the hospital to see J. W. She had to put him in a hospital in New Orleans. She said she'd go there and she'd eat the food off his plate, the food he wouldn't eat, and that'd be her supper. Jackie Lee called J. W.'s father. She asked him, "If J. W. dies, what am I gonna do? Can I send his body back to you?" "No," he says, "if he dies, just dig a hole in your backyard and throw him in it."

# A HOUSEWIFE AND
# A SALESMAN

When we first got married, your father was a salesman and didn't work but two days a week. He was always saying, "Tomorrow'll be a better day." He hardly ever worked on Monday, Tuesday, and Wednesday. He said in the beginning of the week people were so busy they didn't want to talk to you. J.W. sold these great big calendars that went on the wall, you know with a pretty picture and the name of the company on it. Sometimes he'd take me along—shoot, your daddy was a fast talker . . . I know one time we stopped at a little country place on the road and he went in there and he sold two hundred dollars' worth of calendars that day!

Back in those days before you were born things were much nicer and better for me. Your daddy was a humble man in the beginning, we got along so good together. He was very devoted! He was very good! He was very kind! He wouldn't even go down one block to the grocery store and back unless I'd get in the car and go with him. It just seemed like to me we were like twins, we loved each other so much. That's the truth. I looked forward to him coming home and he looked forward to coming home. We were raising a cat, that's the only thing we had, like a baby with fur—J.W. loved that cat like he loved a child. We didn't have much, but it doesn't matter what you've got as long as each of you are happy, and we were happy. Everything was just rosy.

I didn't go no place and do anything, I was just a housewife. I cooked and I cleaned and I washed and I ironed—J.W. was the one that taught me how to iron shirts. He had white shirts he wore all the time with French cuffs, and back in those days all I had was an old wringer washer and the clothes had to be hung out to dry on the line. Everything would get all wrinkly and so there was a lot of iron-ing to do. I'd see him drape the clean shirts everywhere and go 'round with a pot of water, sprinkling them good and then rolling each one up until there were seven rolls waiting to get ironed. Your daddy was always a neat man, always neat and clean as a whistle. He'd put the sleeves on the ironing board and show me, so I got real good at it. I used to have to iron seven shirts a week for your daddy. Old Man Clarkson found out I ironed when he saw J.W.'s shirts, so I started ironing six shirts for him and five shirts for Dewey. Some-times I ironed all day long and then in the evening all I did was get ready and cook supper. J.W.'d always come home about five o'clock—he was good as gold—he would hug and kiss me and almost break my bones. I'd always have a nice meal waiting on the table when he came in. That was my life.

Every Friday night, when J.W. would come home for the week-end, we would run to the grocery store together, get our groceries, come back, have our little meal, and then me and him would go downtown and see a movie. One thing about your father, he was romantic . . . he'd always hold my hand in the movie and he liked me to put my head over on his shoulder. Then on Saturday night we'd go dancing. In those days I'd rather dance than eat. This is before you all were born. When I first started dancing with your daddy it was hard because he was tall. It's hard to believe as short as I was and as tall as he was, how I could get used to him, but I did. J.W. was a good dancer and a good leader and he helped me a lot. In fact I think he, really in a way, taught me how to dance—I mean to dance real good 'cause I knew how to dance and I even won a contest once for the Charleston . . . but he could swing me out and pull me to him and I'm telling you I could wear out a nice pair of dance shoes in one night—he'd never want to sit down—I'd have to come home and throw my shoes away.

J.W. AND LOUISE, MARRIED TWO YEARS, C. 1940

One thing about J.W. though, he sure didn't like me talking to anybody or going out without telling him. I remember one night when we hadn't been married over two or three months and we was downtown going to a show. I saw a couple of boys passing by, you know, friends of mine. They honked and they hollered, "Hello, Louise!" I said, "Hi!" and waved back. Your father liked to die!... he fussed all the way back home. We lived in a small town and I did know people...I thought it would look stupid to not speak to any-body 'cause I was married. If J.W.'d seen somebody he knew, I wouldn've thought nothin' about it if he spoke to them or waved at them. He just thought it wasn't a married woman's place to be so friendly.

## A CUP OF SUGAR

Patricia, when I first got pregnant with you, your father thought I had malaria. He was giving me malaria medicine for about three days but I kept getting sicker and sicker. We didn't understand what was wrong...that's when I went to the doctor. This doctor looked at me and smiled. He said, "You're going to be a mother!" I said, "No, I can't be a mother 'cause I've been married for five years and I can't get pregnant." I couldn't believe it—your daddy and I never ever talked about it. When the doctor told J.W., he looked at me and said to the doctor, "Really...do you think she's going to be all right?"

The doctor said, "She'll be just fine."

"Well, what do we do now?"

I remember the doctor saying, "The only thing you do is go home and be normal."

J.W. kept on asking me, "Are you all right? How do you feel? Are you scared?" I said, "No, I don't feel scared." I lied 'cause I didn't want to worry him — I said, "I just feel like the doctor has made a mistake." J.W. acted like he was very concerned towards me. So we went on home. When we got in front of the house, he made a strange request: "Don't tell Dixie." My neighbor was Dixie Bonds — we lived upstairs and she and her husband, Floyd, lived downstairs. "Don't tell Dixie that you're pregnant," J.W. told me.

"Why, J.W.?"

"Well, she'll probably feel bad . . . just don't tell her anything about our business."

So I didn't tell Dixie and we all stayed very good friends. She never said nothing to me about being pregnant, but she knew I was because as the days went on I got bigger and bigger . . . and I began to crave earrings! You know, like some women crave pickles. Pregnancy seemed to agree with me, but I noticed that your father would go out at night saying he had to go on a call and collect money and the person wasn't there and he had to go back and collect it, and like that. Then one day I was making a cake and I ran out of sugar. J.W. said he would run downstairs to borrow a cup of sugar from Dixie. I heard him run down the stairs and I waited and I waited for him to come back. I finally decided to go down and see what was keeping him. I don't know what made me do it, but I stooped down and peeped through a hole in Dixie's kitchen door. I could see your father with his arms around Dixie, hugging and kissing on her. I went on back upstairs and didn't say anything to him about it. I kept it locked up inside of me.

Then one morning J.W. said, "Louise, would you like to go have dinner downtown and let's us go to a show." I hardly ever went anyplace anymore, so I said, "Oh, yes, I want to go!" We was getting ready to go and the phone rang.

When he got off the phone, I said, "Who was that?"

He said, "Oh, it was just business."

We left the house and after we had walked a few blocks, J. W. said, "Louise, I just remembered I've got to have my tires fixed. This is the only day I will have off and I've got to buy two new tires and have my tires switched and if I take up time going to the show I won't have time to do all this—would you feel bad if I didn't go with you today?"

I turned around and looked at him and I said, "I don't know what you are talking about—you know, J. W., this is very unfair to me."

He said, "I know it is, but I forgot all about it, Louise, try to understand—I want you to take this money—go to the show and I want you to go out to dinner. I don't want you to be disappointed."

I was crying a little bit, we were standing there on the street—I was six or seven months pregnant with you, Patricia. Well, I couldn't convince him, he just kept saying, "There is just nothing I can do about it . . . come on, Louise, be a good sport . . ." He left me standing on the corner. Of course, I felt like I'd lost my appetite. I felt like I didn't want to go to the show. I didn't know what to do with myself. I just stood there on the corner and I watched him go way down the street like I was paralyzed. I saw him go about two blocks and then he darted into this hotel. I crossed the street. I went down to the hotel as fast as my legs would carry me—went through the hotel— went out of the side door and looked to see if I could see him. I couldn't understand where he went. I remember looking up and down the street thinking, I know something's going on but I don't know what it is. Then it dawned on me to cross the street and go into this drugstore and call Dixie's house to see if she was home. Dixie answered the phone.

"Dixie, I wonder if you've seen J. W.?"

She said, "No, I haven't seen him. I haven't got time to talk, Louise. I've got company now and I'm real busy!"

I said, "Oh, really!" and she hung up in my face. Well, when she did that my heart began to beat really fast.

I caught a bus and went out to the end of Broadway—I knew exactly where she had moved! She lived at the back of the Illinois Central Hospital. I got off the bus and went through the IC Hospital yards, crossed the street, went up the steps and knocked on her door. Dixie came to the door . . . she had her blouse all undone. She looked mad. "What are you doing here?"

I was mad as she was! "Is J. W. out here?"

"No!"

In the background, I could see your father running through the house sticking his shirttail down in his pants. I pushed her aside and I went through that house into the back bedroom and walked right up to him. "What in the hell do you think you're doing?"

He said, "I came out here to borrow a book."

"Oh, you did! Well, get your darn book and get out of this house!"

Dixie came back there and said, "Now this ought to be the showdown . . . you tell Louise right now . . . you know what I mean!"

J. W. looked white as a ghost. He said, "Louise, we better go."

Dixie turned to me and said, "Your husband's in love with me and he wants a divorce from you!"

J. W. said, "Now, why did you tell her that!"

I started walking towards the door and I said, "I'm gonna tell you something right now, J. W., I'm walking out that front door and if you don't follow me, I'm gonna keep on going. If you want to stay here with her, it's up to you." J. W. came out there and grabbed me. Dixie came to the door and screamed as loud as she could, "You're nothing but a chicken!"

When we got home, your father got down on his hands and knees and promised me he would never, never do this again. He said, "I don't know why I did this stupid thing, but I love you, please believe me, Louise, I don't care anything about Dixie — I'll never see her again — I care about you, and I want us to have this baby."

# PEACE BOND

You were born. I can remember so well when they brought you in to me. You were a very pretty little round-faced baby. I was so very proud to know you belonged to me. Your daddy at that time was a very happy man and seemed to love you very much. He wanted to name you Tangerine because that was a popular song he liked, but I said, "No, J.W., we can't name that child Tangerine!" J.W.'s father acted so strange when he found out the baby was a girl. At first he wouldn't come and visit, because, he said, "We don't have girls in our family!" That's what he told me, "We don't have girls in our family."

Your father thought he knew everything and I did not know nothing. I remember one time when you were just a baby, you were sick with a very bad cold. Your father had to go off that night and I was alone. My mother told me to put mentholatum on your little chest and up your nose to make you breathe better. I gave you a nice warm bath and put the salve on you and covered you up. I thought I was doing the right thing. J.W. came in about 10:30 P.M. and when he walked in he smelled the mentholatum. He got real mad and jumped all over me and said I was causing you to catch pneumonia. He went in there and woke you up out of a sound sleep and bathed you all over. He always condemned me for everything I did. If you children got sick, he said it was my fault, I'd done something to cause it. I could never do nothing right!

Patricia, your father's promise didn't last long. Three or four months after you were born, I began to see him change back again. He started going out at night, saying he had to go out on a call and collect money—he'd be gone for two or three hours and I'd ask him why it took him so long and he would say the person wasn't here and he had to go back—and like that.

One evening I was sitting there by myself and I got to thinking about where he was. I went to look for your father. I left my baby in the middle of her little bed. She was asleep. I covered her up. She was so tiny. I knew it was wrong for me to do it, but I didn't have nobody to help me—I couldn't ask nobody so I had to do things on my own. I locked the house. I slipped out the back door and walked five blocks down the street to the restaurant where Dixie worked. I waited to see if he would come. I don't believe I stood there over ten minutes and here come his car! Immediately when I saw him drive up, Dixie walked out of the restaurant. I went right over there and I walked right up to that car. When he looked up and saw me he was so shocked he stepped on the gas and shot that car right down the street like a cannon. I ran after him and tried to grab onto the back of the car. I hollered for him to stop, but it didn't do no good. I sat down in the street and cried. I didn't feel no hope. I cried all the way back home. Those days I was always crying...your father didn't seem to care how much he hurt me and I couldn't tell nobody what was going on.

When I got back home, in about fifteen minutes J.W. was walking in the door. He tried to make up to me, throw me on the bed and make love to me. He wanted to do his little dirt and then come back to me for forgiveness, like a child. I didn't go for it! I fought him like a tiger!

I went down to get a peace bond against your father. When J.W. found out, he showed up. He got down on his hands and knees in the judge's office, begging me not to leave him. "Don't do this! Please don't do this, Louise! I'll do anything, whatever you want me to do, I'll do it." I was scared of him 'cause I didn't know what he might do. He kept saying, "I'll promise you anything, but please don't sign these papers! How could you embarrass me like this?" I can hear him right now, "Louise, don't leave me...please don't leave me...I love you." I looked at him and he looked so pitiful...I knew I couldn't do it. I remember...I looked outside, it was pouring down rain. J.W. opened the door and I stepped out into the dampness.

## MARRIED WOMEN DON'T WEAR RED

I wasn't ever allowed to wear a red dress or anything trimmed in red. Your father just always said, "Nothing but whores wear red." I never did think nothing about red till he kept talking about it, then I kind of wanted it. One time I seen a nice red wool dress I wanted. But he says, "Married women don't wear red." I said, "Well, I didn't know that!" I was shocked! One time your father bought himself a brand new bright red wool sweater. I thought, "He don't allow me to wear red and he's bought himself a new red sweater." So I asked him, "How can you, a married man, wear red?" He said people didn't talk about men like they did about women that wore red.

I never did work after I became a married woman, your father didn't want me to, he said he wanted to take care of me. He never did like to give me money. If I needed powder or lipstick or something

LOUISE WITH U.S. PRESIDENTS' PLAQUE, C. 1946

like that, he'd pick it up at the grocery store for me. If I needed clothes or shoes, your father wanted to go shopping with me. We would go downtown, go in the store, and he would let me look and I would go to him and say, "I like this... do you think it looks all right?" I'd try it on and if it fit good, he would pull the money out of his pocket and pay for it — but it was the strangest thing, I thought — a man going with a woman to buy clothes.

I was on the witness stand the whole time with your father. I rarely left the house without his permission — I was afraid. If your father caught me gone he would ask me a thousand questions. He'd want to know where I'd been, who I'd seen, what time did I go, what time did I get back, and all like that — I just didn't want to go through with it. I didn't have any idea how much your father made. I never seen a penny of his paycheck. I knew when he was gonna get paid though, he'd ask me what I needed at the grocery and then he'd always bring in the groceries. I never went to the store with him anymore, he wanted to buy everything himself.

I remember I went to town one morning and he give me some money, which was very unusual. When I got home he said, "Let me have your change," and I give him everything I had but there was a quarter missing. I didn't understand where the quarter was, and he kept questioning me about it. Well, I believe he quizzed me for a half an hour before I realized that when I got downtown the store wasn't open and I didn't know what to do, so I just went in the dime store and had a cup of hot chocolate and a doughnut. I had bought that darn doughnut and cup of cocoa, that's where the money went!

LOUISE, AND PATRICIA PLAYING PHONE, C. 1946

# A WORE OUT DISHRAG

Your daddy was just oversexed! I was naive on this subject, I did what he wanted, what I thought was expected out of a dutiful wife, but it was just like we wasn't meant for each other because what he wanted me to do I didn't like. We would go to bed at night at nine o'clock and he wanted to have sex before we went to sleep and then I'd have to be very careful when I was in bed with him because if my toe accidentally touched his toe he would wake up and want to have sex — it didn't matter what time it was — three o'clock in the morning, he wanted sex. He'd wake up at five o'clock in the morning and want to have sex and then he'd come home at noon and he'd want sex again. I felt like when I woke up in the morning I wanted to be left alone, I didn't even care if he talked to me . . . but he was raring to go. I'd say, "J.W., don't you feel tired?" He said, "We have to do all we can because one day we're gonna get old and we won't be able to do this." Old! We weren't old, but Lord have mercy, way back in my thirties, I felt old, shoot! I felt so old sometimes I couldn't even walk from the bedroom to the kitchen!

J.W. wanted to lay in bed all day! I can remember one time, he'd been home all week long and I kept saying every morning, "J.W., don't you think you need to go to work?" He said, "Well, yeah, I'll think about it tomorrow — maybe I will." He did go to work on a Thursday and I was glad 'cause it would give me a chance to clean up the house and do everything I wanted to do. He left that morning and I was busy getting the house cleaned up, and darn, if I didn't look up and there stood J.W. in the doorway.

I said, "J.W., what are you doing back here!"

He said, "I got to thinking that tomorrow is Friday and it would be a better day to go out on the road 'cause people wouldn't be so tired and they'd have time to talk to me."

But, of course, he came back and all he wanted to do was go back to bed with me and have sex. Later after your brother was born and you all started school, after he'd drive you all to school he'd come back home and I'd have to lay in bed all day with him. The house wouldn't get cleaned up, supper wouldn't get cooked . . . finally he'd say, "You better go take a bath and get dressed, I'm gonna go pick up the kids from school." I'd like to see any woman have sex for four hours a day and then cook dinner and take care of her children and her house! I felt like I was married to half a dozen men. I was a wore out dishrag, that's what I was.

MY FATHER'S WORK WAS MAKING CALLS. HE WOULD SAY, "I'M GOING OUT *to make a call. I'll be gone all day. Come on, Patricia, go with Daddy." One time, as we were driving along chatting, he showed me the alum he kept in his pockets, explaining that it kept his hands dry when he shook hands with his customers. We turned into a parking lot and I was told to wait in the car. Daddy pulled a small amber bottle from under his seat, unscrewed the cap, and put the circle to his lips. Closing his eyes, he leaned his head way back. I watched the liquid move into him. He flashed me a great big smile as the bottle went back under the seat. A clap of thunder broke our gaze, and it started to pour. I watched my father run towards a door that said "Office," his light gray suit spotting with rainwater. I sat obediently waiting in the front seat, feeling safe from the sheets of rain that whipped against the windows. His whistling awoke me. "Grab your coat and get your hat / leave your worry at the doorstep." It was one of Daddy's favorite tunes. I knew my father had made a sale; he was in a good mood. We drove off*

*happily together. The sunshine was glistening through the raindrops, which meant, according to Mother, that the devil was beating his wife.*

MY MOTHER HAD SMALL FEMININE FEET. WHEN THE SHOE SALESMAN TOLD *her she would need a half size larger, she protested and continued to squeeze her feet into the size four-and-a-half sample shoes she had always worn. The first thing she did in the morning was put on her high heels and turn on the large brown radio that stood in a prominent place against the wallpaper's white magnolias. I heard "clickety-click" as she went up and down the stairs to hang the wet laundry outside. My mother and I cleaned, dusted, and danced our way around the house. I tried to keep up as she had taught me to do. The magnolias whizzed by as we twirled to "Green eyes...your green eyes with their soft light..." At noontime, we sat together at the red Formica kitchen table, eating lunch and listening to soap operas. Mother would fix me a pimento cheese sandwich on white bread cut into even halves, and she would have a plate of leftovers from last night's supper. She said that would keep us from having to eat the same thing again that night. The radio dial was tuned to the familiar station that would broadcast her favorite soap opera,* A Brighter Day. *A man's deep voice would tell us: "Our years are as the falling leaves, but somehow we keep hoping, don't we?...that our dreams come true on that brighter day."*

*I knew when it was almost time for Daddy to come home from work; my mother*

Feb 23.1946
House

PATRICIA WEARING LIPSTICK, C. 1946

*would sit at the dresser, take the pink rollers out of her hair, apply her foundation, and dot a black beauty mark on the mole near the right corner of her mouth. When she drew on her red lips, she would reach over and put some lipstick on me, teaching me how to press and rub my lips together so the color would be even. As my father's steps were heard on the back porch, Mother slipped into the two-inch heels that would raise her four feet eleven inches up closer to my father's six feet. She gave herself one last look before rushing through the rooms towards the kitchen door. Her timing was impeccable. Clicking loudly across the bare floor, Mother and I greeted Daddy in our high heels and red lips.*

## A NORMAL MAN

It was the strangest thing, but your daddy and I'd have big fights and fusses—about nothing! And then he'd always go out and buy something—always surprise me. Just like one morning out of the blue sky, two men knocked on the door and one of them said, "Is this the Clarkson house?" I said, "Yes," wondering what in the world . . . and he said, "We got a stove here to be delivered." I said, "Well, we didn't order no new stove." "Well, J. W. Clarkson, Jr., wants this stove delivered." I couldn't believe it, we had been looking at pamphlets and stuff, but I thought we was just dreamin'. I was so happy, Patricia! That evening when your daddy came home I ran through the house and threw my arms around him. He smiled real big and he was happy that he could make me happy. Your brother Davy reminds me of your daddy, I see that same smile sometimes cross his face and I think of J. W. When he'd come home I would always meet him at the door — I called him my big bear and he would call me his little bear.

I was so proud of that stove, it was just like diamonds to me. When we had a disagreement, I got me a nice mixer and one time we had another fuss and he brought in a waffle iron — I still got it in there right now. I've had that waffle iron for forty years. Yes sir, that's one thing I can say he would do!

Then one morning after we had a big fuss the night before, J. W. called and told me he bought us a new house. I remember I was pregnant with your brother Wiley and I was worrying about how we would have room. I kept saying, "J. W., where are we gonna put the baby?"

I remember, your daddy came in that day and told me. "Well, you got a new house!"

"What . . . !"

"I bought a house."

"Where?"

"I'll take you over and show it to you."

"What kind of house is it?"

"Well, it's not a new house but it's got good double floors." That meant it was a good house 'cause it would be warm in the winter.

When I started having my labor pains — of course, your father was on a trip — I called my mother and she told me to call the doctor and she'd be right over. The doctor told me to go straight to the hospital. J. W. got back around 5 P.M., so he was there when Wiley was born around 11 P.M. that night. I barely remember him coming into the room but when I looked up he was smiling.

"Well, we got us a boy!" He seemed very, very, very happy. He wanted to name our son John Wiley III. I said that was fine. Your father was very kind to me after I had Wiley, there was a big change

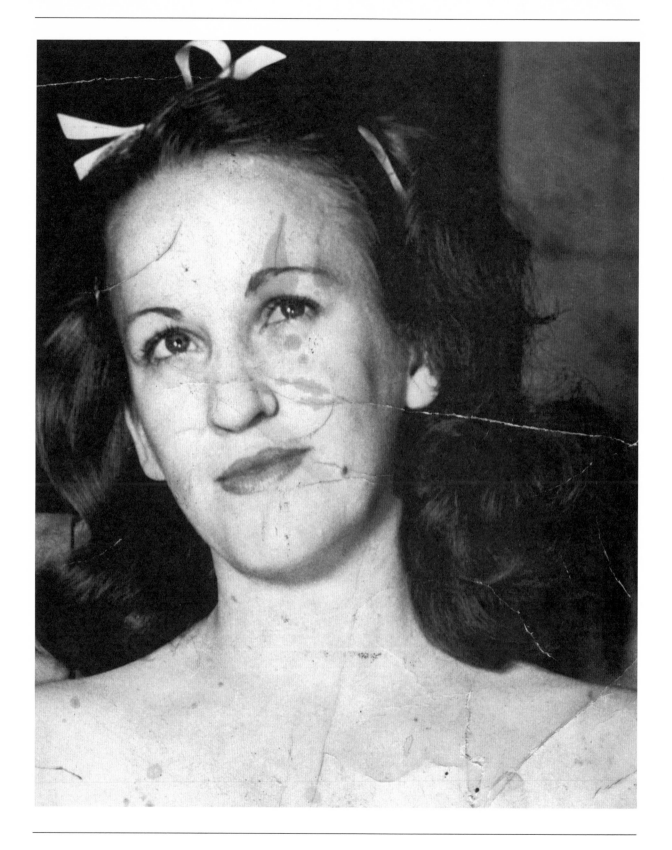

LOUISE, C. 1948

J.W., C. 1948

< SUPPERTIME ON CLOVER STREET WITH UNCLE DEWEY AND MAMA CLAIR, C. 1947
LOUISE HIDING BEHIND WILEY, C. 1947

in him—he couldn't do enough for me—waiting on me around the house.

When we moved into our new home on Clover Street, we spent the first couple of years fixing it up. The first thing your daddy did was set him up a darkroom in that little room off the bathroom. He had maybe two enlargers back there and all kinds of equipment for developing his pictures. The next thing he did was have a double sink put in the kitchen, and then he decided he was going to put some new linoleum in the kitchen and the dining room. He asked me how did I want the living room fixed. Well, my idea was . . . I had a beautiful blue mohair couch and I wanted my walls in royal blue and I wanted all my woodwork white and the venetian blinds white trimmed with blue. So through the Sears and Roebuck catalogue he ordered me some white venetian blinds, trimmed in blue like I wanted. In about two days the room was painted and in the meantime the blinds came in. Then he bought me this beautiful rose rug for the living room. Oh, it was beautiful! Of course, we was very happy.

On the day J.W. was laying the dining room floor he got a telephone call that these people from St. Louis was in town, and he had to quit putting the floor down, go downtown that day and talk to them about a job. A month later they called and told your father that he had a good job if he wanted it, working for United Fire Insurance Company in St. Louis, Missouri. At the time he needed a job real bad because we were only living on our savings.

We got our home fixed up and J.W. had a good job . . . everything was happening for the best for us. We were very happy. Unbelievable. Everything was perfect in our life. Your father was a normal man, doing like a normal man is supposed to do: staying home, working, being good to his family — he got off at night and would do nothing — he was just home and was just a good family man.

KENTUCKY DAM ("LOUISE TOOK THIS ONE" WRITTEN ON GLASSINE ENVELOPE), C. 1950–53

LOUISE BEHIND SCREEN DOOR, HOUSTON, TEXAS, 1989

# 2

## LOVE IS STRANGE

*I arrived in Houston besieged by the anxiety that had become commonplace whenever I visited my mother and saw her subsistence life. My wish to change it nagged at me. The first Saturday I was there, she took me to church with her. Displaying a big smile for everyone who passed our pew in the Seventh-Day Adventist Church, Mother looped her arm through mine so everyone could see how proud she was of her daughter. We held hands as the preacher led prayer. Her hand felt rough and small, her nails chipped and ridged under a layer of cotton-candy-pink nail polish. I closed my eyes and remembered those hands cleaning when I was a child; I pressed my hand closer, feeling protective of my little mother. After communion was passed around, we were all herded downstairs for the ritual washing of feet. I kneeled on the floor below my mother and took her left foot in my hand as she instructed me to do. Her toes all bent to the left instead of going straight ahead, exactly as mine were beginning to do. I held her foot, tightly bound in flesh colored hose, as if it were a rock. I cupped my hand, scooped up the water and poured it over calluses, yellow nails, and dry skin. I was glad for the stocking that gave me some protection from the painful love I felt when reminded of my mother's life of self-sacrifice.*

LOUISE WITH PATRICIA IN BACKYARD SWING, C. 1948–49

# A WILD STREAK

One day a girl called the house and asked for your father. She said she was from Farley's stationery store and she said that Mr. Clarkson's pencil was fixed and for him to come and get it. After he got his pencil fixed I seen a change in him. I noticed he was acting kind of strange around the house . . . going out and coming in at all different times. He started going out on Saturdays . . . he started making trips . . . little things going on.

I started getting suspicious and it wasn't long after . . . we was getting ready to have Sunday dinner and a car drove up in front of the house. I saw a little girl in the front seat and a man, a big tall man, was getting out of the car. When J. W. saw them, he flew down the steps and went right out there. He talked to this man for a long time, I guess over half an hour. I asked him, "J. W., who were those people?"

"Oh, somebody I know," he told me. He came in and ate his dinner. Then he told me, "I've got to go on a trip today. I probably won't get in till late."

I didn't know, I thought it was some kind of business trip. But trouble was coming up on me and I didn't know it. I wasn't ready for it, everything was going so well . . . but your daddy was a salesman, he was out of town a lot. I remember the day I found out.

It was hot and I was in the kitchen ironing your little pink dress trimmed in blue ribbons. You were out playing in the yard—your father came into the kitchen and hung his coat across the chair. Something, I don't know what, told me to go over there and look in his coat pocket. I found a letter, and I could not believe what it said. "I'm sorry I don't love my husband but . . . I think a lot of you but I just can't . . . I can't leave my husband . . . maybe you can leave your wife . . ."

I felt very sad. I could feel tears dropping out of my eyes. I could feel them dropping onto your dress. I put the coat back on the chair, straight, so he wouldn't find it messed up and I took the letter and put it down inside of my brassiere. J.W. came through the house and picked up his coat. He turned around and looked at me. "You took a letter out of my pocket and I want it."

"I don't know anything about it."

"Oh, yes, you do, you've got it and it's not your letter and I want it back!"

There's a lot of things, Patricia, I don't really want to tell you and I made up my mind I wasn't going to tell you what happened that day. I'm afraid you're going to think your daddy is crazy . . . 'cause I think he was crazy. It was real hot that day, all the doors and windows were open. He was fussing, arguing, hollering, screaming, carrying on. See, I didn't want to give him the letter until I had finished reading it. I went out there and sat on the front porch—I thought if I got away from him, he'd finally calm down . . . but he didn't . . . I remember Wiley was sitting down beside me, he was about one year old—he was so little.

J.W. threatened me, he said, "If you don't come in this house and give me that letter back, I'm going to tear up your suit." At that time I had a brown gabardine suit that I loved. But I was stubborn, I just sat there on the steps and ignored him. I thought he was bluffing. A few minutes later he went through the house and he walked out on the front porch that day with my beautiful suit and began tearing it all to pieces. When I saw what he did I got more determined than ever not to give him the letter.

He said, "Okay, if you don't give me the letter I'll show you what I'll do!"

He went in there and took a knife from the kitchen and he cut up a good leather chair. It was a beautiful yellow chair — he upholstered it himself. When he did that I got up . . . 'cause I knew he was crazy . . . and I took the letter and threw it in his face.

He took the letter, got in the car and left. I felt like he was somebody I didn't even know. It must have been something terribly wrong with me for him to treat me the way he did. I was a good person, a kind person, always willing to try to help people. Your father was very easy to be led off — nobody could have influenced me to stray away from my family, I could be in a room with two hundred men and they could flirt with me but they wouldn't have no effect on me because I always knew my place. I guess you'd call me a straitlaced person. I married J. W. to be a wife and a homemaker and that's what I wanted to be.

I look back at my life now and I think the only reason J. W. wanted me around at all was he needed somebody to raise you children — he needed somebody to keep house — he needed somebody to be like a slave and he wanted to be the wolf. Sometimes I thought J. W. hated women. I felt like he went out with other women to spite me. When I asked him what made him do the things he did, he always said, "I'm just like my mother, I got a wild streak down my back."

One time I counted all the women your father went out with and there were twenty-two, that I knew of. I didn't know all their names but they were brunettes, every one of them, I know that much. Your father was stuck on himself. I had to tell any woman I met to be careful and don't look at my husband a second time because he'd get the idea they were flirting with him. They'd always laugh and say, "Okay, we'll be careful!" I couldn't never have friends. I guess you could say your father was like what you call a Don Juan. But you know—it's the strangest thing, everything your father did he never believed in—

no, he never did. I can remember him going to bed with a Bible in his hand. He'd sit on the bed and read—sometimes he'd say something to me about what it said. He thought that when you're married, you're supposed to be married—he would talk about men he'd hear about, you know, that was ratting around on their wives, or getting a divorce—it was terrible, he thought. He would say, "Oh God, that's just terrible, why would they do that"...and then he turned round and done it himself.

MY FATHER ONCE RESCUED ME FROM DEATH. I HAD DEVELOPED A HABIT *of swinging so rapidly between the arms of two chairs that I would lose my breath and turn blue. One of those times, my great-grandmother, Big Mama, screamed, "Louise...!" Louise screamed, "J.W....!" J.W. screamed, "She's gone!...we've lost her...!" My father grabbed me up and rushed to the kitchen sink. My head was held under the cold running water. After a hard slap in the face I began breathing again. Big Mama put out her warning: "Louise, you all have got to watch this child, she is going to kill herself!" Mother wrinkled up her forehead. "I know, but what can I do!" Raising his voice, my father gave the orders: "Louise, get rid of all these chairs with arms. I want Patricia watched twenty-four hours a day — we don't want to lose our little girl!"*

*When I was sick, my mother traded comics for me with the neighborhood kids. Trying to please was her aim in life. Other people came first, she told us. She had an innocent nature and was never in a bad mood. She never hollered at us or got angry about anything. She made us fudge and Rice Crispie treats; when it snowed, she made ice cream, adding sugar to the scooped-up back yard snow. Mother liked to surprise us with new furniture arrangements. Using her hip with great determination, she could move large pieces of furniture an inch at a time, huffing and puffing all day until she was satisfied. Daddy joked that he was afraid to come in at night, as he never knew where it would be safe to sit down. Once she cut the posts off the antique four-poster bed; another time she painted the blond bedroom set black. Arriving home from school, we would reward her. "Oh, Mother, this looks so much better, we love it!" Every day was a new experience. Neighborhood kids loved to come to our house, at least when Daddy wasn't home. When he was there, we had to be vigilant soldiers, alert to his mood swings. Mother called him a Dr. Jekyll and Mr. Hyde.*

## FLAT-CHESTED

Well, I began to watch him . . . On Saturdays he always had things to do. I didn't think too much about it during the daytime, but on Saturday night when he'd get himself all cleaned up and go out, I knew that something was going on. Then, one day, I answered the phone and a strange man said, "Do you know where your husband is?"

I said, "No, I don't."

"He's out with my wife."

"Who are you?"

"I'm Norma Granger's husband."

LOUISE IN CLOVER STREET BACKYARD, C. 1948–49

"What are you telling me—?"

"Don't you wonder why your husband's been going off at night and staying late and you don't know where he is?"

"I thought he was working."

He said, "I'd like to see you and talk to you because I imagine we have things to talk about—would you meet me out?"

I went out and met him. His name was Asher. He said J.W. had been going out with his wife for quite a while. She worked down at Farley's stationery store. I couldn't believe it—how could I not know anything about this woman—I always knew...

He told me his wife wouldn't have nothing to do with him, wouldn't talk to him. She wouldn't cook his meals and when she'd get in bed at night she'd sleep so close to the edge she could fall off and hit her head on the floor. He was suspicious so he followed her, and that's when he found out about J.W. He asked me, "When are you all going to get a divorce?"

"Well, we've been getting along just fine. There's nothing wrong with us..."

"I'm afraid my wife got the idea he was going to marry her."

I said, "Well, we're not talking about no divorce!"

He said, "I just think you better watch him because my wife has already went down and sued me for a divorce. I came by here that day to ask your husband to leave my wife alone. He claims that he's not having anything to do with my wife, that they're only friends, that he just met her down where she works and he's not having no affair with her and I don't have nothing to worry about—I don't believe him!"

So, Patricia, I decided to go down to Farley's stationery store and see this woman. I got myself all dressed up nice and I walked in there and I asked to speak to Norma Granger. So she came around and I'll never forget how she looked. There wasn't nothing glamorous about her at all. She had an old long skirt that looked like it was almost down to her ankles. I never will forget that. She didn't have no breasts. She was flat-chested as she could be. She had kind of an old face on her. She looked like she was mad at the world. I walked up to her and I said, "I have been told that you're going with my husband, Mr. J. W. Clarkson, Jr., and I want you to know that J. W. and me have been married for twelve years and we are not in the process of no divorce. I don't know what you're doing or what you're up to, but we have a family—we have two children—I'm telling you to leave my husband alone!"

She said, "Well, John said you all weren't getting along and was getting a divorce, but don't worry about it. I don't think I'm gonna leave my husband—I have a little girl—he doesn't want me to leave him. I'll break this up, don't worry about it." Then she asked, "Could we meet out someplace besides this store? I'd like to talk to you more about this." I wasn't interested in talking to that woman! I said, "I don't have anything to talk to you about! I'm just telling you to leave my husband alone and if you don't I'll be back down here."

J. W. threw a conniption fit with me because I went down and saw this woman. That day I had put on a blue chiffon dress with little red flowers in it 'cause I wanted to look my best when I went down to Farley's. We were fussing and I was standing in the doorway, and he said, "You don't have a slip on!"

"Yes, I do!"

"Well, you're gonna have to put two slips on 'cause I can see through your dress."

He was telling me what to wear and he was out running around with a woman! Your father was a very strange man—after this big fuss about Norma, the next morning we were driving in the car, and he looked over at me and said, "Louise, the way I treat you, did you ever think about trying to beat me up?"

I said, "No, that never entered my mind!" I saw him reach back and pull a sewing machine belt out of a sack, and he said, "If I give this to you, will you beat me up?"

"No, I won't!"

"If you loved me you would."

"I don't know what you call love, but I'm not going to do it!"

"If you treated me the way I treat you I'd want to beat you up."

"Well, you have different thoughts in your head than I have — I'm not going to ask you to beat me up!"

"Why wouldn't you want to do it?"

"Because I don't do things like that!"

"I bet you I could ask other women to do it and they'd do it."

STANDING ON THE SIDEWALK IN FRONT OF MY HOUSE ON CLOVER STREET, I *could see the coal stacked high in the Illinois Central railroad shop yards, the place where the trains went for maintenance, repairs, and overhauls. Across the tangled brush and swampy lot we called the hollow near the alley off Madison, lived my best friend, Daleanne Trimmings, a strong-willed, fearless six-year-old with long, straight hair the color of straw. Daleanne had it good at home. Her parents, Charlie and Mavis, never said a cross word to each other. Mavis smoked and was the boss in the house. My mother held Mr. Trimmings in high esteem as a good provider. Charlie thought my mother was every man's dream woman. "A good looker," he would say. "The hardest day's work J.W. Clarkson ever put in was the day he married Louise!"*

*Daleanne and I were the only girls in our neighborhood. We each had a bossy streak. The boys drank our concoctions, ate our mud pies, and followed our commands when we played army. Daleanne and I were inseparable; she was more like a family member than a friend. I believe she thought she lived with us since she was there most of the time. She'd take liberties I wouldn't have dreamed of. My father could be in the bathroom shaving in his jockey shorts with the door closed and Daleanne would barge in, sit on the toilet, and stare up at his fully lathered face while her hot pee splashed down below. Daddy would just laugh. It didn't seem to bother him. It was her idea that we use my father's good silk ties as halters, modestly tying them around our chests to cover the two brown spots we knew to be different from the ones we saw on the bare chests of Dennis Benton or Bobby Hughes. Daddy never said anything about that either.*

*The more I loved my best friend, the more power she had over me. A favorite argument between Daleanne and me was whose father was better than whose. She would say, "My father's better than your father, my father drinks beer!" I would retort, "No, my father's better than your father, my father drinks whiskey!" I couldn't seem to win an argument. We could doggedly disagree, up to a point, and then the fear of losing her would grab hold of me and cause me to lose ground. When she knew she had me, she would stick up her nose and stomp off towards home. In the same tone of voice I heard my mother use, I would run after my friend and beg her not to leave me.*

PATRICIA TRYING TO POSE AS DIRECTED, C. 1949

WHEN I WAS SEVEN YEARS OLD AND A MEMBER OF THE BROWNIES, MY *father would pick me up from my after-school troop meetings. One afternoon while I was in charge of plopping the spoonfuls of cookie dough exactly right onto the waxed paper, I caught sight of him in the cafeteria doorway. I wondered what he was doing there so early. Then I saw my Brownie leader, Mrs. Hughes, walking towards him. My father's face was turning into a bright red tomato. He was grinning like the Cheshire cat. I felt the urge to throw my body flat out there on the linoleum, tripping her and averting their meeting. Why did other women besides my mother have to exist? My father was a magnet of flattery. I knew what was going to happen. He didn't seem to notice me as I pretended to be caught up in the multiplying greasy peanut butter balls. After that Daddy began coming early and loitering around the door talking and laughing with my teacher, who was his type, as Mother said, a brunette. Unlike the other daddies arriving in casual after-work clothes to pick up their little daughters, mine would be all dressed up looking like he was going to a party. He embarrassed me. After all the other girls had gone I sat in my Brownie uniform studying my catechism lesson, being ignored, while he flirted and carried on with my teacher.*

*One day after school as I was gathering up my pencils and books to go to my Brownie meet, Sister Rose Henrietta came to my desk and said my mother was on the first floor waiting for me. At the top of the stairs I looked down to see my mother's worried face. I knew what was coming. "Patricia, I'm sorry, honey," Mother said.*

*"I know what you're thinking, but your daddy said he don't want you going to the Brownies anymore. He doesn't like your teacher, honey. You know how your daddy is now, don't cry, there's nothing I can do about it."*

*Mother looked beautiful that day. I remember her hair smelled fresh, of Prell shampoo. She was wearing a long-sleeved sky-blue dress, belted at the waist, with little black bows and pearl buttons. Her lips were fragrant and scarlet. Her eyes pleaded with me not to make things worse, to do as I was told. She helped me with my chocolate-brown sweater, which matched my tan Brownie uniform, and slipped her fingers through mine. My mother held on so tightly that I wondered whether I was holding her hand or she was holding mine. I could hear my friends downstairs singing. As we rounded the corner I saw Daddy's green Dodge. "Patricia, I know what's best," my father said. "Your teacher's not fit to be a Brownie leader — there will be other things — you have lots of time . . . I know what's best."*

## THE HOUSE IS PERFECT

It was that summer of 1950 that your father met Norma. He got in deep with her very fast. He was working all week in St. Louis, and every weekend when he came home he was going out with her. It seemed like it was excitement for him to know this woman. I guess she was just like him — she'd do everything he wanted her to do — I

LOUISE HOLDING WILEY, C. 1950

J.W. HOLDING WILEY, PHOTOGRAPHED BY LOUISE, C. 1950

guess some women are like that. It wasn't no secret. He knew I knew it. I told him I wanted to have the truth—I wanted to know where he was—I felt like I deserved something. But it just seemed to make him worse once he knew I knew.

He hadn't had that job for United Fire Insurance Company over two months and as soon as he started making good money that's when all this happened. I call it showing off with his money. I didn't know what to do! What I believed in was a dream. I kept thinking what he was doing wasn't gonna last long. I had in the back of my mind that if I stayed home, took care of my kids, was a good home-maker, looked after my family, that one day I could break him down and he would come back to us. Because whatever he did J.W. always said, "I love you—just give me some time—everything will work out." I believed him. I was living on a dream and I wouldn't listen to nobody. Although I knew they were right, I wouldn't listen to them. I was trying to protect him.

When your daddy would come home from St. Louis, I was always really happy to see him and it was a comfort to know that he was inside the house. All the time he was gone I worked like a dog—I killed myself—I cleaned venetian blinds, washed windows, waxed floors. I wanted to impress him. I wanted to have the house so clean and so neat and everything so absolutely perfect that when he walked in there wouldn't be no excuse! Mrs. Mallory, my next door neighbor, said she'd never seen anybody work so hard as I did—she came in and said, "The house is perfect, Louise . . . just perfect!"

Right before your father was supposed to come in one weekend, he called and said he didn't know for sure if he could come on the Thursday like he had planned. Anyway, I kept on cleaning on the house . . . getting things fixed and polished so everything could be perfect when he come in. I looked for him all day on Thursday, but he did not show up. Friday passed. On Saturday I cooked a nice dinner, thinkin' he might come in sometime in the late afternoon. I stayed up till after eleven o'clock that night.

When I was asleep, I heard a noise in the house and turned on the light. It was twelve-thirty in the morning. The house was perfect. I raised up in bed, I put my arms out to him to kiss him...he was very cold. "Where've you been, J.W.? Why are you so late? Why didn't you call me?"

"We had a bad flight...I left late..."

"How do you think the house looks?"

"Oh, I didn't even notice."

"I worked awful hard to get this house clean so that you would think it looked nice when you walked in! J.W., where have you been?"

"I don't want to talk about it. I'll talk to you in the morning! Leave me alone, I want to go to sleep!"

"J.W., why don't you lay over here close by me and let us talk for a little while."

"No, I'm tired—we can talk tomorrow." He turned over and in a few minutes I could hear him snoring. That next morning, it was Sunday, when he got up he went out back and washed his car real good and cleaned the inside and everything. When he came back in, I said, "Why don't we go to the park? It's such a beautiful day." You children ran through the house and jumped up and down. "Yes, please, please, can we go!"

"I've got a trip to go on today—I'll be in late tonight—I've got some business to do."

"I don't believe you! How could you plan on a business deal when you just got back home?"

"Well, something came up that I can't do nothing about and I've got to go."

Very independent like, he went out the door, with me begging him, "Please don't go! Please don't go!" I was so hurt—he just didn't have no feelings. I didn't know what to do. I felt like I'd like to leave. I felt like I was by myself. I didn't want you all to know how hurt I was. I didn't have, really, no one to turn to—I couldn't have many friends—ever since my father died, my mother had a hard time making ends meet, so she moved to Fort Worth to be with her sister, Aunt Dahlia. I felt like I couldn't be calling her and telling her about my problems.

I know now it didn't make no difference if I kept a clean house. He didn't care if the dirt piled up to the ceiling, but I thought it was good for me to do this. He kept saying, "You think I care that when I come in, the house is clean! I don't care! I'd like for you to sleep all day long and get your rest and make yourself feel good and not even clean anything so that when I come in you would feel like talking to me and being with me instead of worrying about this darn house! I don't care about the darn house!"

DADDY WAS GOING OFF TO WORK, AND MOTHER STOOD HOLDING THE *door. The intense early light jumped around my parents' darkened shapes, carving them into cardboard cutouts. Daddy looked like a magazine picture in his finely tailored suit, standing tall and perfect with his briefcase. Mother, barefooted, was in her plain print cotton housedress, her hair still in pin curls. I saw her lift her head slightly and purse her mouth. Daddy tilted his head downward and their lips briefly met. My father smiled at me as he turned and walked away. His long dark lashes framed the bluest of eyes, fragile like fine crystal, telling one story while his mouth told another. Mother stood watching at the screen door as*

LOUISE SWEEPING BACKYARD, C. 1949–51

*Daddy slipped into his green Dodge and then disappeared down Clover Street. I thought it was exciting the way he could drive away from dirty dishes, carpets that needed sweeping, and a messed-up house that showed remnants of last night's fussing and fighting — Mother had thrown a Coca-Cola bottle and even a hot skillet right off the stove at Daddy when he came in late from his date. "Love is strange," I thought. I looked forward to the time when I could have my own car. As Daddy rounded the corner out of sight, Mother turned and walked directly to the kitchen sink, immersed her hands in the lukewarm dishwater, and with her fingernail scraped the dried egg off my father's breakfast plate. Our day had begun. Daleanne was skipping in the back door and we were off to play.*

*By the age of nine, Daleanne and I were arguing over boyfriends. "He likes me!" "No, he likes me!" One day, my mother, sick of listening to our spats, offered to solve the disagreement by going to the chosen boy's house and telling him to write the name of the girl he liked best on a piece of folded paper. She walked the two blocks down to Bobby Hughes's house, knocked on his door, explained to his mother why she was there, and succeeded in getting Bobby to write his answer on her paper. When I saw my scrawled name, I got scared because I thought Daleanne would beat me up when she found out. At my mother's suggestion, Bobby was invited to come over that afternoon for a snack. As we were sheepishly munching on chocolate cake, Daleanne included, my new boyfriend tried to kiss me. I socked him in the nose so hard that his blood dripped red onto the dining room linoleum.*

*I felt gratified that I had defended myself against Bobby, but Mother was horrified.*
*She rushed him to the bathroom sink. I can still hear her shrilling, "Why, Patricia,*
*why did you do this! I can't believe you did this! Daleanne, why did Patricia do this?"*

## PUPPY LOVE STUFF

Your father used to have a habit of locking you children out of the house. I would always say, "Please . . . J. W., don't! I don't want to lock the kids out of the house!"

On Sundays I wanted to go to church so bad, I would get up at five in the morning to cook my dinner so I could go and get back in time to get it on the table by noon, 'cause that's when your father wanted to eat. When I got home this one day I started fixing dinner to put on the table and for some reason J. W. insisted for you kids to go outside and play. When you all left, I saw him lock the door. He said, "This is a good time for me and you to go in the back and make love." In a few minutes you all were knocking on the door. You poor little children! I heard you all say, "Mama, why can't we come in?" He said, "Go tell them you have a headache."

I didn't go for this way your daddy had about wanting to have sex whenever he wanted to. In the beginning I was flattered — then after you all were born, I thought it was time to be different, I felt like I was a married woman, I had kids and I thought this was all puppy love stuff and my mind wasn't on it. This wasn't being a mother! This wasn't being an adult! It was like he was a teenager.

I don't know where you children could have been sometime,

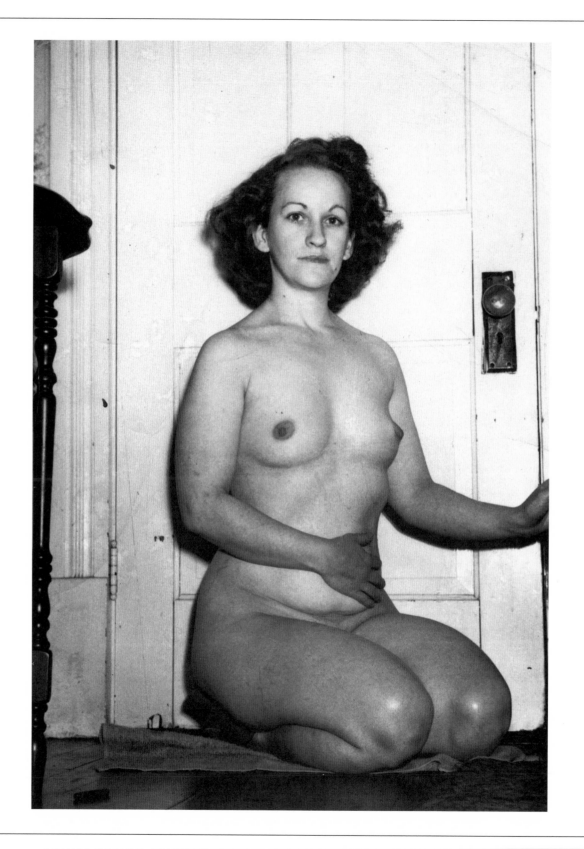

LOUISE POSING AS PINUP FOR J.W. IN FRONT OF BEDROOM DOOR, C. 1950

'cause I sure wouldn't want y'all to see the kinds of things that went on around the house. Your daddy liked to make pictures of me. It was a game with him — he would catch me — I could be laying down with a headache and he would want me to pull up my dress for him to make a picture. He got a big thrill out of figuring different positions for me to do. He liked to photograph up my dress when I was sitting on the front steps. He'd want me to climb up on his car and put my leg up higher. On a trip with him once, he had me lay down in some weeds for him to photograph me pulling up my dress. He took a picture of me sitting up on the radiator. He acted like he owned my whole body. I'd always say, "No, I don't want to, please don't do this to me." All the time I'm begging him he would tell me to "hush . . . be quiet." Your father had a way of talking people into anything! If it was green and he told you it was black, you'd end up saying it was black. I didn't feel like sitting up and posing! I think he had an evil mind and I didn't. I was a very shy person. J. W. was like a big city man and I was like a little country girl. I was a person that believed that there was a time and a place for everything. But he set his own time, he was master of the house and I had to do what he told me to do. He'd always throw it in my face: "Well, if you don't do it I bet I can find somebody that will!"

OURS WAS A SEXY HOUSE. I FOUND A PICTURE IN THE DRESSER DRAWER *of my father nude, lying on the sofa. He looked odd with his Johnson sticking straight up, like a medical illustration of a human abnormality — goiters, hernias, and such lumps, sticking out from what had once been a smooth landscape of skin. Afterwards, whenever I saw my father I thought of the picture. Sleuthing around the house looking for photographs of naked people became a favorite pastime for*

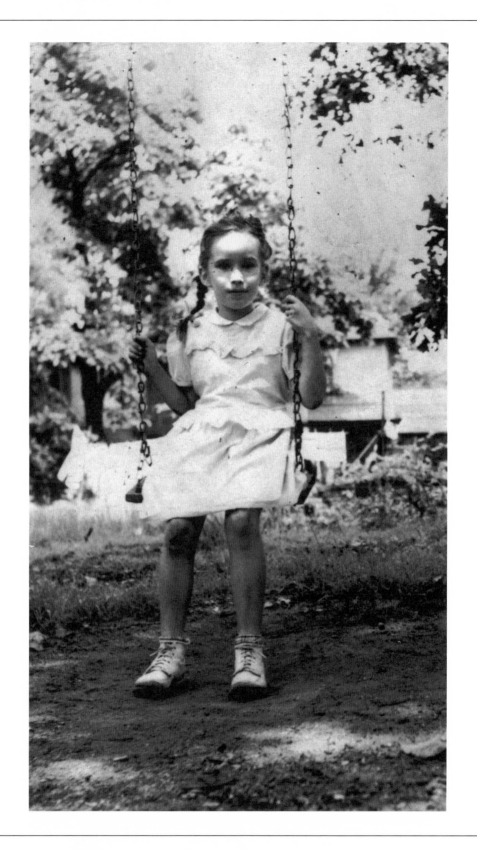

PATRICIA, AGE EIGHT, C. 1951

*my best friend and me. We became diligent detectives and learned that the sexiest place in the house was my father's darkroom or the filing cabinet that he had forgotten to lock. Daleanne loved to say that Mr. Clarkson was the first man she had ever seen without his clothes on. While the neighborhood kids snickered and giggled at her illustrated announcement, I pretended to be distracted and uninterested, sometimes untying and retying my shoelace or picking the thread that hemmed my dress until it unraveled.*

*When my father wanted to lock the doors, Wiley and I had to go outside to play, sometimes being plied with promises of ice cream or a drive if we did as we were told. Once we were on the porch, the dead bolt snapped into place. I was thrown into a panic. I ran to the back door. It was locked. The shades were drawn. I ran to the front door, and my little brother and I beat on it with our fists. "Mama, Mama!" we cried, but no one came. We would hang around on the front porch bickering like two alley cats. We could never leave our post — other kids might come and ask us to go play, but we declined all offers. We needed to stay ready to leap into the house just in case the door opened. As neighbors passed, we thought that they were assuming that we were bad children being appropriately punished.*

*Our mother would finally come to the door and say apologetically, "You kids come on in now." Daddy would be in a good mood, kidding me about being such a sourpuss, tickling Wiley in his ribs, laughing and grabbing Mother. When I saw him touching her, I felt sick and repelled. My mother warned me about sex, saying, "Wait till you see what you're gonna have to do when you get married!"*

LOUISE, C. 1950–52

# A SECOND CUP OF COFFEE

I noticed your father was acting nicer around the house. You know, he'd stay home and sit down and read the newspaper or he'd come up and ask me, he'd say, "I'm going to the grocery store—is there anything you really need for me to pick up?" He was real attentive to me and I knew that when he got that way there was something on his mind, something was going on that he was trying to hide and he was feeling guilty.

One Sunday morning we were sitting at the kitchen table and drinking coffee and he kept watching me. He looked real funny, like a little boy, like he'd been very naughty and he'd done something. He said, "Louise, can you give me a second cup of coffee?" I got up and give it to him and he was still watching me—I could just feel his eyes coming right through me. "J.W., what's the matter? Are you in some kind of trouble?"

"No, not exactly, but I do have something I need to talk to you about...I've got myself in a terrible spot and I need to ask you a favor but I'm afraid you won't do it. I don't understand why I do the things I do—will you please help me?"

"Well, what can I do, J.W.?"

"I don't understand myself...but I need your help...would you call Norma up on the telephone and tell her that you and me are married?"

"Why in the world would you want me to do that!"

"I have made her believe that I'm going to marry her this afternoon and she's over to her sister's house with her hat on her head waiting on me to come over there...I'm in a spot! She's been planning all week long—she's bought a new dress and a new hat and everything."

I said, "For crying out loud, why would you let her do that! Are you losing your mind! What's wrong with you!"

"She was driving me crazy for me to marry her. I decided to make her believe that I would—now today's the day!"

"Well, you better tell her!"

He said, "I need your help—she's going to get mad and scream on the phone, but tell her that you just found out that I was going to marry her and just say that you're sorry but I can't marry her because I'm married to you." So he took me to a phone booth—we didn't have a phone at the time, he had it disconnected so she wouldn't call him—and I called her up. J. W. sat in the car.

I said, "Norma, this is Louise. I just found out you're planning on marrying J. W."

She said, "Yes! I'm standing here right now and he's late getting over here!"

I said, "Well, I just called to tell you that I'm sorry but J. W.'s married to me, he can't marry you at all."

She turned around to her sister and I heard her say, "Well, well, that lemon! He's not going to pull this trick on me, I'll get even with him!"

When I told him what she said, he started laughing. You know, a mischievous laugh, like: "So what!...I promised her and I didn't." I don't know what was wrong with him!

PATRICIA AND WILEY, 1952–53

MOTHER SAYS WE WEREN'T A "REAL" FAMILY BECAUSE WE NEVER DID *anything all together. However, I remember suppertime and our Sunday drives. We would pile into J.W.'s car, and he would drive us through the park and the cemetery, down Broadway to the river front, and back home. During the drive we were careful not to ask for an ice cream, or to stop and feed the ducks, or even to go to the bathroom. If we asked for anything my father would get angry and turn the car around and take us back home.*

*On a typical drive, our parents, sitting polar opposite in the front seat, would begin arguing. To them, argument was conversation. Mother would criticize Daddy's bad behavior. The fussing would escalate. We children would sit in silence on the back seat, afraid to make any sound that might fuel the fire. Mother would grab at Daddy, hitting on him as he was driving. He would slap her. She would jump out of the car and go running down the road. Daddy would drive halfway off the road, get out and grab Mother's arm, physically persuading her to get back into the car. Meanwhile, passing vehicles would swerve to avoid hitting our car's rear end, which was sticking out into the road, and people would crane their necks to see what was happening. Mother would be crying. Daddy would be grim and silent. The day would be ruined. We would all go back home. With the door barely open, they would resume their fighting, turning up the radio to drown out the noise: "It's the Amos 'n' Andy show, folks . . ."*

WE MADE NECKLACES OF CLOVER AND RINGS OF LIGHTNING BUGS. WE *played hide 'n' seek and red light—green light. When we heard the trill of Mother's voice calling us in for the evening, we made a beeline for home. If I saw Daddy's car in the driveway, my body would stiffen at the thought of suppertime.*

*Mother had to have hot bread on the table every night or Daddy would slam his fist down and scare the daylights out of us. No white bread, he told her — biscuits one night, corn bread the next, then hot rolls the following night, and so on. Mother always took pride in putting a nice meal on the table — fresh yellow corn cut off the cob, hand-peeled mashed potatoes, canned beets with vinegar, fried pork chops, hot biscuits made from scratch, and brewed ice tea with lemon wedges neatly arranged on a saucer. I said the grace I had learned at St. Mary's Academy. We weren't Catholic, but my father said a parochial school was the best and that's where I went.*

*My mother's face took on a worried look as she watched Daddy fill his plate. Picking up the plate of perfectly browned and rounded biscuits, touching one lightly to be sure they were hot enough, Mother extended it in his direction. Without a word, three biscuits were missing. "You got enough corn, J.W.?" Mother asked in a serious tone. "Louise, this tea needs more ice!" My brother and I sat quietly, believing it was within our power to hold back our father's imminent bad mood. We couldn't forget the Thanksgiving when Wiley had asked Daddy to pass the gravy and Daddy almost threw the bowl at him, slamming down the spoon so hard that the*

*gravy splashed out all over the tablecloth. Wiley never asked Daddy to pass any-*
*thing again. Mother looked out for us, making sure we had everything we needed;*
*then she served herself. If Daddy wasn't getting mad about something, it was so*
*quiet around our table that the forks and knives could be heard scraping against*
*the plates. We thought that if we were quiet we would cease to be a problem for our*
*father, and that he might feel peaceful and be quiet, too. He would ask, "What*
*are you kids so quiet for?" "Nothin'," we would answer.*

## "WALKING IN MY SHOES"

It was really like I was alone with you all—your father was in St. Louis all week working, and on the weekends he would come home but, like I said, he would go off again. I never had money and to get money I would return all the empty coke bottles. I found out I could stick the hose from my sweeper down in the floor furnace and suck up the school money you all dropped down there. I would clean off all the dirt and find dimes and nickles and quarters—in the summertime that's how I did it.

When J. W. started running around with Norma I think he felt guilty, so he began giving me money to buy groceries and a little money on weekends to take you all to a show. I was used to him going to the grocery store and doing everything for me—then when I had to be on my own I had to learn how to handle money, but it was so sad the way I had to do it.

Your daddy would put thirty-five dollars in my hands to buy groceries, and I'd take you all with me to Piggly Wiggly. I'd buy the meat first. I wanted to make sure I had the meat. I'd bring all the meat up to the cashier and pay for it. I'd have you and Wiley go over and sit down there in those chairs and hold my bags. I'd tell y'all that I had to go back and buy some more groceries and for you all to sit there and wait for me. Then I'd buy all the vegetables I needed and go pay for all of them. Then I'd put the bags down beside you all. I'd go back and get my bread and my cereal—whatever. I would look at my money and count my money and I would try to figure out how much more of it I had. See, I wasn't used to buying groceries—I wasn't used to putting money out. I didn't know how far thirty-five dollars would go. I was in fear of running out of money. I didn't want to be embarrassed if there wasn't enough. You all were so good, you would just sit there and wait for me and never say a word—never cause me no trouble. That's what I did . . . I did it for a long time like that.

Your father started interrogating me bad when you started first grade. He had done it lots of times before. J.W. was the kind that would what you call browbeat me. We started to have fights and fusses because I couldn't remember. I would tell him something about where I'd gone or somebody I spoke to and he would wait maybe a whole month and he'd come in one day and he'd ask me to repeat the story while he looked over his notes, you know, trying to catch me in a lie.

"When you went downtown last month, you told me that you seen so and so standing on the corner. . . well, what time was that—?" I tried my best to remember, but he'd say, "That's not the way you told it the first time—you must be lying." I would say, "No, I'm not lying—there's nothing to lie about!" He would say, "Well, look at it like this, if you're telling the truth, you'll tell it the same way—you won't change. Why don't you just break down and tell me the truth,

Talked to
I called
She called
Clothes on
outside
I called
10:05 —
She calle
had anot
I called
got mad
Clothes
Wash them
anything
Clothes

Tuesday

– at 8:25 – She called me

– at 9:10 AM –

– hacked 9:40 AM & said
ixboard & she was going
hang out

– at 10:00 AM & talked until

– at 10:30 AM & said she
load to hang out – Pants –

– head at 10:47 AM & she
cause I questioned the
– The time it took to

– At 10:05 she didn't say
not washing any more

because you know if you don't tell me the truth, I'll keep on asking you till you do tell me the truth." J.W. was a good teacher. He told me, "When you leave, look at the clock and when you come back, look at the clock." I learned to remember.

Patricia, that's the way your daddy was. I'd say to him, "I don't understand it—I don't need to know these details about you, what makes you this way?"

"I don't know what makes me this way , but this is the way I am and that's the way it's gonna be . . . I'm the type and you're not . . . I just like to keep notes." Then one time when his mother was visiting us, we were sitting on the front porch in the swing and she looked over at me and she said, "My God, Louise, you're living your life like I lived mine! To be here and to see you and these kids, I feel like I'm living my life all over again. You are walking in my shoes! What you're going through I went through with J.W.'s father—J.W. is just like his father!"

Jackie Lee told me that Old Man Clarkson was mean and stingy to her and that after they were married and she gave birth to J.W., it wasn't long before he would never take her no place and there was always fussing and fighting around the house, and she said that all he wanted her to do was stay home and have kids for him. To hear her talk, in her younger life, when she was married to your grandfather, she was in prison. "He would not ever give me no money or take me anywhere. He would not give me nothing! He would go to work and lock me in the house, I couldn't even get milk if I needed it for the children. I got tired of staying home taking care of babies! One day I cut holes in his pockets and when he'd walk across the floor to go out the front door, all his change would fall over the floor." She said she got down on her hands and knees and picked it all up. "I bought flour, grease and sugar and made pies and cookies and cakes and I sold them in the neighborhood." That is how your grandmother told me she did it.

EARLY ON IN MY FATHER'S AFFAIR WITH NORMA IT CAME TO MY MOTHER *that she needed to be more sophisticated, that this might be what her husband wanted in a woman. Her best friend and next door neighbor, Peggy Parker, advised Mother to dress herself up and join her husband for a cigarette. One morning, the egg growing hard on the breakfast dishes, Mrs. Parker decided to give my mother her first lesson on how to smoke a cigarette.*

*"Okay, Louise, hold it between your two fingers like this . . ." Louise drops the cigarette on the floor. They both giggle. "Okay, then, try holding it like — yes, like that" — Mother tries holding it as she has seen my father do it — "between your thumb and that finger" — Peggy patient and seriously instructive — "is that easier? Okay, now when you see the match strike, lean forward and put the tip right into the flame" — striking match — "Now! Too far — back" — helping a little with her hand — "pull in! Pull in — suck, suck — suck in, suck in — quick, quick!" — coughing violently, Peggy patting her on the back — "Here, drink a little water."*

*"I can't believe you're supposed to pull that smoke inside you," Mother gasps, putting on a look of repulsion that reminds me of Lucille Ball taking a gulp of castor oil. The two of them start laughing convulsively. Finally my mother says, in a low strangled voice, "I don't think I can do it. I can't pull that smoke up inside of me!" Tears streaming down her face, Mrs. Parker is jumping around, holding herself to keep from peeing in her pants. Now Mother is dancing around with her friend, weeping or laughing; I can't really tell. "Oh, you can, you can —*

LOUISE, C. 1950

*Louise, now watch me — look, just pull in a little, then suck a little more, slowly, and then try to catch it before it goes too far down, and — blow it out...like that — okay? — come on, try it again...suck in..."* Mrs. Parker tried hard and Mother did learn how to hold the cigarette in a convincing manner, but she never could quite get the hang of holding in the smoke and drawing on the cigarette fast enough to keep it from going out.

*One morning when my father lit up his cigarette after breakfast, Mother grabbed one of his Kools and lit up, too. Daddy laughed, saying he thought she looked funny with a cigarette. Mother let her Kool burn up in the ashtray, and Daddy went off to work, having shown hardly a hint of interest. I thought it exciting how different my mother looked with a cigarette instead of a broom. I liked her better that way. I wished she would really smoke instead of pretending, but she never did.*

## A HOTEL ROOM IN ST. LOUIS

Your father was always tricking me. One time he said he wanted me to come to St. Louis on a Thursday and drive back home with him on a Friday. He said, "I'll take you out for supper and maybe we'll have time to go out for a show." He said for me to make my arrangements and he would meet me at the bus station. I was happy to go —

it was exciting for me! I was a nervous wreck, trying to get my things together to go on a trip. I remember I got all dressed up. I put on a big black picture hat and I wore my gray suit and my gray suede high heels. I had on white gloves. I thought I looked real good. I kissed you both goodbye — I can't remember who took care of you all.

I didn't get up to St. Louis until it was practically dark outside. When the bus pulled in, J.W. was standing there...I remember so well. He wasn't very affectionate that night. He just said, "Did you have a good trip?" When we got to the hotel the elevator had broken down and we had to walk up ten flights of stairs to his room!

We sat around in his room and talked for a few minutes — just what was going on at home. Finally I said, "You know, it's getting late, are we going to go out someplace and try to get a bite to eat?" He said, "Well, could we stay here for a little while and talk? I want to ask you to do something for me."

"What is it?"

"I've got some papers that I've got filled out...I want you to look them over and I want you to sign them."

"What are the papers about?"

"Well, say in case...I'm not saying it will ever happen, but in case me and you ever separate...I think I deserve Wiley and you deserve Patricia."

I said, "What are you talking about!"

"Well, in case anything ever happens...I want you to sign Wiley over to me and you can keep Patricia."

"No, I'm not signing Wiley over to you!"

"Well, he's my son!"

"He's my son too, and I'm not going to turn him over to you! I'm not signing no papers to give you custody of my child! No, I'm not, J.W.!"

"Why do you want to be so selfish? Norma's got a child and I haven't got nobody. You want both kids and it's not fair!"

LOUISE POSING AS MODEL FOR J.W., C. 1950

EASTER, C. 1951–52

"I'm not selfish — they're yours and they're mine, and if you want them you're going to have to be with me! You're mixed up with this woman and you're telling me all the time everything's gonna work out. It's not gonna work out and I'm not gonna give you Wiley!" We sat and argued from seven o'clock till four in the morning. I was hungry! I was thirsty! I was disappointed! I was wore out!

Early that morning when he finally let me climb in bed, he wanted to turn over and have sex with me. I slapped his jaws! I would not have nothing to do with him! So he turned over on his side and went to sleep and so did I. I woke up in the middle of the night and I said to myself, "If I had money I would get out of this room . . . I'd disappear and he wouldn't be able to find me." But I couldn't go, all I could do was lay there and cry. I never told Wiley this story.

That next day your father and I drove all the way back home to Greenfield. He didn't have hardly anything to say to me and I didn't have anything to say to him. I felt like I was so alone I didn't know what to do. I was so glad when I walked in and you kids acted like you loved me and were so happy to see me. I don't think your father was capable of loving children or of loving me.

THERE WASN'T MUCH TO DO IN GREENFIELD AND WHATEVER THERE WAS, *Daddy thought we shouldn't be doing it. For entertainment, my mother would take us to church and to the movies. I never knew what religion we belonged to. Mother was a Seventh-Day Adventist; Daddy was a Methodist; I went to Catholic schools; in the summers I attended the Baptist Vacation Bible School; we enjoyed going to the Episcopal Church's potluck sociables. (Mother's perpetual potluck dish was pea salad: canned green peas, squiggles of red pimentos, little squares of Velveeta cheese, chopped onions and lots of mayonnaise.)*

*On Sundays, we would get dressed up and go to some church. Daddy never went, but he would drive us right up to the front door of whatever church we were attending that week. After we had our Sunday dinner, my father would go off "on business." As he drove away, Mother would ask us, with anticipation in her voice, "Patricia, how would you and Wiley like me to take you to the picture show today?" We'd yell, "Yes, yes!" The house had to be cleaned first, and then it was our turn. After hot baths, with our hair combed, shoes polished, and clothes pressed, the three of us, hand in hand, would happily trot along the edge of Barkley Avenue, cars whizzing by, making our way into town, a sixteen-block walk. We'd go to the two o'clock matinee; with news, serial, comedy, and feature, half the day could get used up. If Mother had extra money, we'd go across the street and have a Walgreen's Supper Special.*

*One evening my father was supposed to pick us up from the movies at six o'clock. Mother stood by the door of the theater looking for Daddy while Wiley and I watched the movie two more times. He didn't arrive until close to midnight. After the movie theatre had closed for the night, we had to stand outside and wait. Mother explained that there wasn't any more money so we couldn't take a cab, and it was too late to walk.*

*I felt ashamed standing there on the deserted street of Greenfield's downtown with the manager of the movie theatre looking and wondering what was wrong. When Daddy finally drove up he was red-faced and all smiles. His windows were rolled down like it was the Fourth of July — we were freezing, standing and wait-ing, hopping and skipping. The marquee brightly announced* Bad Day at Black Rock. *Daddy acted like nothing was wrong. Mother, looking incredulously at him, began asking where he had been and what he had been doing. The fireworks continued through the night.*

## A DIVORCE

One day, J.W. came home and said he wanted a divorce. He hadn't been going out with Norma very long, it just seemed like everything started getting real serious real fast. I guess he made a lot of promis-es to her. He said, "I want you to go down to so and so, down on Broadway, at a certain lawyer's office and be there by two o'clock in the afternoon." I could not believe it . . . I thought I was dreaming. I knew that things was bad, but I didn't think he'd want a divorce. I went downtown that day and I went in this building . . . I climbed that big flight of steps — it was like up to the moon, it was so high up. I went in this office and this lawyer got up and offered me a chair. He leaned over and said, "Mr. Clarkson wants a divorce." I don't remem-ber exactly what he said he wanted the divorce for. I think the word was compatible. Well, I don't know why I did it, but I started crying and the man got up and sat over by me.

He said, "You know, I want to tell you something. The whole time Mr. Clarkson was talking to me, he told me what a nice woman you were." He said, "Mr. Clarkson is prepared to give you your home

and two hundred dollars a month." So when the divorce started coming up and I knew that he was really gonna do it, I asked him, "When are you planning on leaving the house? Why don't you go ahead and get an apartment? Does she know you are still living here?"

He wanted things to go on like always. He told me, "Louise, don't worry about nothin'! Don't say nothing to nobody and don't let nobody know I'm living here!" It was odd, because during this time, J.W. was nice and kind around the house and I can remember just before we got the divorce, he put a furnace in the house and, you know, he was doing things for us as if we was gonna be together.

The day the divorce came through I'll never forget. Early one morning I heard my next door neighbor, Mrs. Mallory: "Louise, you have a phone call!" (J.W. didn't want a phone at home, 'cause, he said, he didn't want no trouble from Norma.) I went over there and it was the lawyer on the phone. "Well, Mrs. Clarkson, you're a free woman, your divorce has been granted!" The minute I walked back in the house and J.W. found out that we was really divorced he acted scared. He said, "Louise, don't you leave this house!"

I said, "No, I want you to leave!"

"No, I'm not gonna leave. I never did want the divorce anyways. I only wanted to get a divorce to show Norma that I could do it so she would get off my back." He said, "I want you to drive with me across Mississippi and we're gonna get married again. Let's leave right now and try to get back before Patricia gets home from school."

"J.W., you have to be crazy! What is wrong with you?"

"Louise, I love you, I never did want a divorce. We can't afford to get a divorce. I love you and I love the children and I want us to keep our home . . . but I had to prove to Norma that I could get a divorce."

"Something's wrong with you, J.W.!"

"Louise, we can't break up our marriage, we have too much! I promise you, just give me some time and I'll work this out."

He always made promises and, you know, I believed him. I don't know why. I guess I kept thinking things would work out and be different... he would settle down. Even when he was running around, if I needed anything around the house, all I did was say, "J.W., we need so and so," and he'd say, "Okay, tomorrow I'll get it."

Well, all right then, we got ready and got in the car. We took Wiley with us and drove to Corinth, Mississippi. We got remarried there at this nice little church. J.W. was just thrilled to death. There was a lady and a man and a preacher there. He hugged and kissed me right in front of them. The preacher asked us, "Is this your second marriage?" And J.W. said, "Yes, we've been married before but we've had some trouble and we're going back together and try to make it." The preacher said, "Well, I'm always glad to see things like this happen." On the way back we stopped someplace and had a little picnic. Then we went straight on back to Greenfield.

J.W. acted like he was so happy that we went back together. He'd walk up to me and put his arms around me and say, "Louise, I do love you — I don't know what makes me do the things I do — please just bear with me until I can work all this out." That Christmas was the best Christmas I can remember. Your daddy bought you that beautiful dollhouse. I remember he got so excited. He got down on the floor and put all the furniture inside, and he was so happy and I was so happy, we couldn't hardly wait for you to see your doll. He gave me a beautiful set of silverware — Wiley got his first tricycle and a Roy Rogers cowboy outfit and holster set. You all were thrilled, of course, you all thought Santa Claus had brought these things.

I know, Patricia, you keep wondering why I married your daddy again — I didn't know what else to do. I didn't know how to go out and make a living and take care of you all, 'cause you were very young at the time, Wiley was four and you were eight. I was scared to be out by myself. I didn't know how to face the world! I never had no

experience at nothin'! It's awful for a woman not to have no training, fighting to stay alive and hoping every day of her life that things are gonna get better.

THE SOUND OF MY MOTHER'S CRYING CALLED ME TO THE FRONT PORCH. I *sat down on the swing, to her right, and Wiley was on her left. We moved closer, with our arms around her, while we watched Daddy pull out of the driveway. "Your daddy is leaving us and it is my fault. Your father wants a divorce and I'm to blame, your father don't love me, that's what's wrong . . . when a man don't love his wife he can't love his children either." I believed it was true as Mother told us, that it was because of her that our father didn't love us anymore. I built up a secret resentment toward her, believing that she was at fault for all the mess we were in. She wasn't doing something right — she couldn't keep the house cheerful, she couldn't keep Daddy at home, she couldn't make him happy. My mother looked at me and asked what she should do. I didn't know what to tell her — I was nine years old. I tried not to cause her any more trouble than she already had. I took charge of Wiley, preparing him for bed, choosing his clothes for school, and watching out for his safety. I sat quietly, listening and comforting my mother as best I could. Once I heard my father say, "Louise, don't be telling Patricia all our troubles, she's too little for all that, she needs to be out playing with dolls not listening to these things!"*

# PLAYING ROULETTE

Your daddy's company insisted that he move his family to St. Louis. He was still living in that hotel there and they had been paying for it, so he had to make arrangements for us to go. He promised, "After we're gone, Norma won't know where we are, and we'll get this thing straightened out. We'll make a new start—just trust in me and believe in me—don't tell the kids, they might tell somebody, don't talk to nobody—neighbors—*nobody*!"

On Sunday nights when he'd go back there he'd take little things in the car like glassware or lamps or I'd fix a box of pictures, things we didn't want the people in the moving truck to carry. So your father invited me to St. Louis to show me this house he had rented for us. Well, it was a cute little house in a nice neighborhood. The day I went in there I noticed a broom and a mop and dust rags and it looked like maybe somebody had been washing the windows. I said, "J.W., who's been here? Who's been doing all this?"

He said, "I don't know, I guess the landlady has been up here trying to clean up the house a little bit." I thought, well, that made sense, that could be. Your father went out and bought sandwiches and cold drinks and we had a little picnic down on the floor in the empty house. We talked about how we would decorate the house and how lucky we were for J.W. to have this good-paying job—you all could be put in private schools—and we were just real happy that day.

Then the time kept getting closer and closer for us to go and one day he said, "We're gonna have to slip away and not let Norma know where we are . . . if she finds out, I might lose my job."

Well, the day finally came, and it was time for us to go. The Mayflower moving company came with a big long truck and they backed it up into our yard all the way to our door. I remember J. W. coming to me early that morning and saying, "Louise, pack a bag, we will have to go to a hotel and stay one night. I am going out to my father's house, but I'll be back in about an hour." So the truck kept getting filled up. When the truck was about half full, the phone rang. It was J. W.'s boss in St. Louis. "Oh, Mrs. Clarkson, I've got bad news to tell you! I've received a phone call from the main office — my boss in New York has told me that something was happening with J. W. and his family and they didn't want no part of it and that J. W. had to be dismissed. A woman called the New York office and said that J. W. was ready to marry her and that he was taking his ex-wife up to St. Louis."

See, Patricia, your daddy must have told Norma he got divorced, but we got remarried and she didn't know that. J. W.'s boss said, "Mrs. Clarkson, I'm very sorry... this has hurt me, I thought so much of J. W. It's just nothing that the company can do and you better just go ahead and unpack your things and tell J. W. that I will be in touch with him later." I knew I had to go out there and tell the men that they had to bring our things back in the house... that's when I broke down and started crying because I knew that we couldn't get away. I didn't believe he'd ever give her up.

In the meantime, before I could do that and before J. W. could ever get home, the phone rang again, and it was the lady that owned the house in St. Louis. "I'm sorry Mrs. Clarkson, but I just found out that you was having trouble with your husband, that he was involved with another woman. She just called me and told me she had been cleaning up the house because he promised her that he was gonna move her, but that she found out he was gonna take his ex-wife."

I said, "We're trying to get away from this woman — we're trying to make a life of our own!"

"I'm sorry, honey, I think you're in a lot of trouble, but I can't rent my house — I can't trust Mr. Clarkson."

About a half an hour later, your father finally walked in the back door. "*J. W., we can't move!*" J.W. stood there like somebody hit him in the face with a piece of pie! I started crying again and your father looked like he was ready to have a nervous breakdown. "Louise, go tell these men that they're going to have to start putting our furniture back in the house." I remember J.W. wouldn't go out there and so I had to tell those men that something had happened and we couldn't move. They kept saying they were sorry and so they brought everything back in the house. They did it pretty fast and everything was very, very sad. I remember you and Wiley was standing there and you didn't understand what was going on.

What I didn't realize was that your father was playing a double game . . . like a roulette, that's what I call it. He admitted that he had made Norma believe that he was going to take her and her daughter, Tory, to St. Louis. He said, "I didn't intend to ever take her — I just made her believe it to get her off my back." He had gone over to Norma's, and when she found our overnight bag in the back of his car, she was so mad that she ripped up all our clothes and then called his boss. I said, "J.W., this could never work out, you promising her and promising me — what were you thinking!" This was the end of everything.

The day was passing. We didn't know what to do, then we remembered all our little knickknacks and stuff that he had been taking up to St. Louis all these months. J.W. said, "What can we do, we'll have to go up there and get them." I can't remember who I got to take care of you all. We got in the car and drove to St. Louis. There wasn't much feeling. There wasn't much spoke between us. We drove, we drove . . . in my mind I was thinking that maybe this time, it was all over with this woman. I know what you're thinking, Patricia, but he was my husband and I wanted to believe in him. I thought, when you marry, it's for life. It don't make any difference what the man does to you, you're supposed to stay firm. I thought it was my duty to be good to my husband, and I felt like if I did, it would make him feel bad when he'd go out, he'd be thinking about how good I am. This is ridiculous, I know now.

All the time we was in the car I kept talking and asking him, "Are you going to give her up? Are we going to get our life straightened out? You've lost your good job, now we don't have nothing! You can thank Norma for everything that's happened!"

"I know, I know, but that's all right," he said. "I'll get even with her!"

We drove practically all night long and I fell asleep in the car — we got up there very, very late. His hotel room was absolutely a storage room, loaded with lamps, dishes, pictures, mirrors, odds and ends that he had been carrying up there. I wondered how in the world we was gonna ever get all of it back. We went straight to bed 'cause we both was dead tired, and early that next morning your daddy went and got a trailer and we loaded up all of our things. I felt sorry for your father — I did, he just looked so beaten. He had to go over to his office to unload his desk and turn in his keys. He really was embarrassed but he had to do it. I sat on his bed and prayed that somehow God would help us through this bad time. He was gone for at least a couple of hours — he came back and he didn't say anything but I knew it was all over.

We drove all that night trying to get back to Greenfield. We got back early that next morning . . . I remember I had to go over and get you all. You all was very confused. The house was a wreck. I didn't know what we was going to do. Sometime that next morning J. W. said to me, "I don't want you messing with this house today — I will help you tomorrow. I want you to go downtown and go to Finkel's and pick you out a suit and buy anything else you want — I don't care what it costs." I decided that before he changed his mind, I better go do it. I went down to Finkel's and I found me a suit that I liked and it cost me fifty-five dollars back then. I bought me a pair of brown shoes and a brown purse and I was really happy. I got home late that afternoon — I can remember it was in the wintertime 'cause it was getting dark. J.W. was already home. When I got back in the house, I noticed that your father was in the bathroom — he stayed and stayed, so finally I knocked on the door.

I said, "J.W., What do you want for supper?"

He said, "I don't want any supper."

I couldn't understand what in the world he was... all at once I began to smell some kind of lotion, like a man's aftershave lotion for his face.

"J.W., what are you shaving this time of day for?" I began having a funny feeling inside of me. I said, "J.W., you're not getting ready to go back to that woman, are you!"

He said, "I'm going out on business."

"You are not going out on business — you're going out on monkey business, that's what you're going out on!"

He started to put on his shirt and I pulled it and it ripped. He pushed me and I fell on the bed. I started to cry and he grabbed a shirt and his jacket and ran through the house — I ran after him and when I got to the living room I could see him getting into his car — he was pulling out of the driveway.

After he left, all I could do was just break down and cry... I knew that things was pretty bad. I looked around me and all I could see was that dirty, tore-up house, boxes sitting everywhere and my two poor little kids. I remember you all sat around me and looked at me and put your arms around me and you couldn't understand what was going on and I couldn't explain to you all what was going on in my life.

Things was getting worse and worse with us. Your father seemed like a very weak man. He always seemed like he was going to do his

PATRICIA AND WILEY ON CLOVER STREET FRONT PORCH, C. 1951

thing and I was like a pair of old shoes up on a shelf, and he needed to be able to reach up there and know I was there, just in case he wanted me.

WILEY AND I HAD LEARNED THAT IF WE HAD TO SNEEZE OR COUGH, IT *was best to run from the room and plunge our heads into the bathroom hamper or a pillow, anything we could find to muffle the sound. If my father suspected any ill health, he would inspect the ailing body part under a lamp, quarantine us from play and school, and make us lie for endless hours under a tent of vapor inhalant, or, worse yet, blame Mother for being the cause of it.*

*I had a nervous condition which made me need to pee all the time. When the need welled up, I would stoop and press my heel hard into the urgency. At school I purposely dropped my pencil on the floor and then stooped down to pick it up, staying there until the need disappeared. When I got a wet spot on the back of my skirt, I twisted it around to the side and carried my books down low so it was hidden. My teacher, Sister Rose, told me I didn't have to raise my hand when I had to go; I could just look at her and, when she nodded her head, I could be excused to the girls' bathroom. That way other kids wouldn't know. Afraid that he might blame her, Mother had been hiding my problem from Daddy. He found out after I had an accident in the First Baptist Church Sunday School room, where I sat petrified after everyone had filed out, the pee stinging my legs, the smell choking me with fear. While I was plotting a quick silent escape, a man came over and looked at me kindly. "Young lady, can I help you home?" I was handed over to my father, who stayed home from work the next day to take me to a specialist. The two men conversed above me. The doctor jokingly diagnosed my problem as "the busy little girl" syndrome — "too busy on the playground to stop and relieve herself," he told my father. They both laughed.*

## THAT MOVING MAN

I had gone down to the drugstore to pick up a notebook you needed for school the next day, and when I came out, one of the Mayflower moving men was passing by in his car. He stopped and spoke to me and I spoke back. He said, "I'd like to find out what happened on that move of you all's — I felt so sorry for you — the truck was almost filled up . . ." I don't know what made me do it, but I sat down in his car and told him everything, and then he wanted to bring me home. I said, "No! No! My husband wouldn't like that."

By the time I walked home — it was a long ways from that drugstore — your father was there. He was on the porch and he started raising hell when I came up. "Where were you! Why were you down there so long? What were you doing? I want the truth!" When I told him the truth it made him raging mad! He said he was so upset about me being gone because he had brought me a present home and he thought he would surprise me — that he came home early especially to bring me this present and I wasn't there.

I looked around and I said, "Well, what was the present you brought me?"

He said, "I brought you home a nice mop and mop bucket."

Can you believe he'd say that to me? I should have took his mop bucket and put it on top of his head! I wasn't nothing but a washer-woman! That's all I was! No, it made him jealous for somebody to talk to me! He liked to have killed me for talking to that moving man!

Your father was so evil that that night he went in there and threw me on the bathroom floor. He took all my clothes off me and examined me just like he was a big doctor to see if I'd went out and had sex with this man. I was screaming! I was crying! I was telling him I hadn't done nothing and I was trying to get away from him.

He called the Mayflower moving company the next day and somehow found this man. I heard him on the phone. "I want to know did you touch my wife?" I was so embarrassed, but I couldn't do nothing. After that night, for almost two weeks, ever once in a while he'd come in the house and he'd get to thinking about it and I'd see him go to his filing cabinet and pull out his notes and he'd write notes just like you, Patricia, and he'd have questions to ask me: "Where'd you meet him? How long you been knowing him? How long's this been going on?"

See, J.W. could do anything he wanted to, but I could never do nothing. If he caught me standing out talking to anybody, he'd question me for days, months, I'd never hear the end of it. He had me so programmed, I couldn't talk to nobody!

I BELIEVED IT WAS OKAY FOR MY FATHER TO QUESTION MY MOTHER AND *to punish her, just as we children were punished when we were bad. My brother and I sat in the living room listening to my father question my mother about this man she was seeing. No one thought of turning on a light, so we sat in the dark. There was no supper. My father commanded that we go to bed, and, as he took me by the arm to push me towards my bedroom, he tore my dress. I carried on about my favorite dress. "Oh why, oh why, Daddy, did you tear my dress?" In my room I tried to press the cloth back together, but it was ruined. Crying and worried about my dress, I tucked my brother in at the foot of my bed. Wiley and I half slept, listening all through the night to the rise and fall of our parents' voices. I did not dare truly sleep; I had to stay alert to help my mother when she needed me. I heard her pleading for Daddy to stop. "Leave me alone, J.W., I've told you everything I know . . . let me go to bed . . . I'm tired . . . please, J.W., . . . the children . . ." Dozing off and then waking, I heard noises — scuffling, things falling, something hitting a wall, furniture being pushed, my mother crying. When I sensed my mother's danger, I opened my door and ran into the hallway, demanding, or rather begging, "Please, Daddy, please stop hurting Mother!" My father said, "Get out of here, Patricia, go on back to bed now, this is between your mother and me." My mother tried to walk away, but my father grabbed her arm while she struggled to free herself. I screamed, "Please, Mother, please answer Daddy's questions!" "Patricia, go on to bed . . . your mother is okay . . . go on, do like I say . . ." My mother continued*

PATRICIA WITH BIBLE, C. 1951–52

*her pleading and crying, and when she tried to go to bed because she was tired, I heard my father drag her back. In my room, I worried. How could I make my dress not have a tear in it?*

MAMA CLAIR, MY MATERNAL GRANDMOTHER, WAS SURE TO SHOW UP *whenever she caught wind of my mother having trouble with my father. She would arrive by cab, smelling of pancake makeup, pills, and prescription ointments. Following Mother's example, we stood by to be of service to my grandmother. "Come on, you kids, pick up those grips and drag them on in here," she would demand. Fort Worth, Texas, was two days away by train, she told us, and she was "plumb downright worn down from this trip" and had a headache besides. "Louise, what on God's earth are you doing standing there with a broom? Every time I see you, you've got a broom in one hand and a mop in the other — I've never seen anything like it!" "Mama, why didn't you tell me you were coming?" "Why should I, here I am!" Mama Clair would say. Her commands were made in a half whimper: "Patricia, honey, get me a BC from my grip, that little one over there." My grandmother gave the impression of being a big woman; though she wasn't but five feet five inches tall, she had substantial girth, which was tightly corseted and moved about as if she were being pushed forward from the rear. With her elephantine legs and swollen feet strapped into patent leather, she filled up the space of what before had seemed to be a large living room. Her body flailed out, partly on the couch, partly on the floor.*

*My mother was already standing by with a glass of water. My grandmother opened the thin folded paper with the BC headache powder, and, eyes closed, tilted her head way back and dropped its contents into her opened mouth. As my mother supported her head, she parted her lips to receive the liquid. Choking and coughing, Mama Clair yelled, "My God!...Louise!...you're going to kill me...! Hold my head higher...! What's the matter with you!"*

*During these visits, there was a fair amount of competition between my father and his mother-in-law for my mother's time. My mother rushed about trying her best to please everyone but not really ever able to please anybody. "My goodness, Louise, you are slow! I could have had this house cleaned up lickety-split! Throw that spread on over here, you don't need to worry so over it, you're just going to get in it and mess it all up before you know it." Mama Clair taught me how to stave off wrinkles and sagging skin. Digging deep into the economy sized cold cream jar, she scooped and slapped the greasy, white substance, thick and shiny onto her face. With long sweeping gestures, she instructed, "Always push up, up, up. Never down!" she warned.*

*She advised my mother on how to handle her husband. "I would get myself a rolling pin and when my husband would come to the front door at night, I would stand behind the door and hit him on the head when he walked in." That was how to take a man in hand, my grandmother said.*

I OVERHEARD MY FATHER CALL HIS MOTHER A "WHORE," BUT, TO ME, *Jackie Lee* — *Mama Lee, I called her — was a fairy godmother, a woman of poise, style, and class. Every birthday, Christmas, and Easter, I received a beautifully wrapped box. Inside was a dress, jacket, coat, or suit made specially by Mama Lee, with her label sewn right into it. In the winter it was velvet or taffeta and, in the summers, organdy or dotted swiss. My father's rantings and ravings about his mother were meaningless to me; he screamed that she was "man crazy" and had run off with a pots and pans salesman who stole all her money and jewelry and then left her in Kemper, Louisiana. My father liked to tell about how in his childhood he had stood on the porch as a lookout for his mother to warn her when his daddy was coming home so she could stop talking to her boyfriend on the phone. "I know how women are!" he would yell. My mother only had to stand on the same sidewalk with a man and my father would be suspicious that something was going on.*

*When Mama Lee came to visit us, it was as if the queen of England were gracing our humble house with her royal presence. Mother slaved away with preparations, washing curtains, waxing floors, polishing up the silverware we never used, putting away the jelly jars, and getting out the company glasses. Mama Lee could do no wrong as far as I was concerned. She fixed my hair and tied bows in it, and, at night, she sat on my bed reading me stories. The first chance I got, I would slip into the guest room and secretly look through my grandmother's belongings, touching her clothes and her shoes, trying on her jewelry. As I felt the softness and fineness of these objects, I was curiously excited and in love with the woman who wore such things.*

I FELT MY FATHER SLIPPING AWAY. IN MY LOVE FOR HIM I REACHED OUT *my arms in protection. I feared that he walked along the same precipice of mental illness that his youngest brother did. Uncle Dewey was an odd man with white, baby-soft skin who wore ill-fitting clothes and leaned to one side, favoring the leg not affected by polio. He carried his Bible around with him and, like my father, laughed a lot. Dewey had a breakdown when his father died, leaving him a rather large inheritance. With Old Man Jackson barely cold in the grave, my uncle went south to find his mother. My grandmother, Mama Lee, was afraid of her son. She told us he acted strange, that he would come up silently behind her and frighten her. He watched her, she said. She thought he had come to kill her for leaving him when he was a baby. When she asked him to leave, he returned to Greenfield, threw away his inheritance, and began his decline into mental illness. That's when he came to live with us. I was never scared of my uncle, even when he came into my bedroom at night and just stood there while I pretended I was asleep. He was in and out of hospitals, while my father wearily tried to convince everybody that Dewey was just upset about his father's death. When Uncle Dewey refused to blink his eyes or swallow food, he was committed to Martinsville, the local insane asylum.*

UNCLE DEWEY IN WESTERN KENTUCKY HOSPITAL, C. 1961

*The letter stamped "The Commonwealth of Kentucky" said that my uncle had been given the diagnosis of schizophrenia, catatonic type. It said that he could "communicate some, answering 'yes, ma'am' or 'no, ma'am' but with no logical relation to the questions asked."*

AFTER HE LOST HIS JOB, DADDY WAS AROUND THE HOUSE A LOT. MOTHER was hanging out our wash in the dark, saying that she felt funny around the neighbors. With everything still packed up in boxes, Mother announced that we would be going to a new school. It was all arranged; we were moving out to Big Oak to live next door to Loretta and Verle, my best friend Daleanne's big sister and her husband. We considered Big Oak to be way out in the country. Our new house sat on Mimosa Hill, so named because of all the mimosa trees in the front yard.

*Family life got better for us there, for Wiley and me especially—we found new friends and wild outdoor things to keep our minds off our parents' problems. A weathered shed deep in the woods next to an old Indian cemetery got transformed into a playhouse. We covered the walls with snakeskins, and we made decorations from odd rocks, bird skeletons, arrowheads, and old bottles we found. No grown-ups knew of our hide-out. On Saturday nights a bunch of us girls met in the driveway, wearing our white sleeveless pressed blouses and dirndl skirts, and joined the boys from up and down the road for a three-mile hike to the drive-in movies. We took a short cut through the woods, jumping a high creek and going illegally*

*through a golf course (country club property), then crossing a major highway so we could slip in the back way and not have to pay. Sometimes Loretta drove the car with us kids hiding under a blanket behind the back seat or in the trunk. Priscilla, our Native American neighbor, taught us not to wear underwear so we could squat and pee in the high grass even when the boys were around. We watched Bill Haley and the Comets as we sat in the open air under the big screen of Chief Long drive-in, named after the Chippewa chief who led his braves in battle on the very same land.*

*It was a special time for everyone. Mother and Loretta canned and made jam from the blackberries thriving all around the fertile terrain surrounding our house. Berry picking was something all the women liked to do. We wrapped our ankles and necks with kerosene-soaked rags to keep the snakes away and wore long-sleeved shirts, long pants, high socks, gloves, and scarves tied around our heads. Filling bucket after bucket, eating as we went, we moved slowly through the thorny bushes with great care so as not to disturb one of those great rattlers we had seen whizzing through the tall grass along the road.*

*Daddy was a gardener, clumping around in work boots and straw hat, filling crock after crock with cucumbers, and then making pickles — sweet, sour, dill, and relishes, too. In the evenings, sitting around the dining room table where smells from supper lingered, the screened doors and windows flung wide open to let in the cool air, Mother and Daddy played canasta with Loretta and Verle. It made me so happy to see my parents doing something together.*

# MY NEIGHBOR, LORETTA

Things were always going downhill for us and it seemed like every place we ever lived, J.W. always tried to get in with some woman. One time out there on Mimosa Hill, Loretta and I were canning together and she said, "Louise, don't worry about me—I know about J.W.—you can trust me. I know what all you have gone through and I would never mess around with him." I said, "Well, Loretta, I'm sorry to say it, but be careful, don't ever look at him the second time 'cause if you do he's going to get the idea that you are trying to get in with him." We both laughed about it.

J.W. used to like to invite Loretta and Verle over to the house to play cards on the weekend. One night, I saw J.W. trying to put his feet all over Loretta under the table. I hit him in the leg and I think he knew what I meant and he took his foot off hers. Later when they left I said, "J.W., why are you so friendly, with your feet all over Loretta? That doesn't look right at all." "Oh," he said, "I didn't realize I'd done it." Or something like that—some excuse. He was always so insistent about inviting them over to eat on Sunday and we always had plenty so I would invite them and we became very good neighbors. I liked them both very much.

Late one afternoon, it was getting kinda dark—I walked up on Loretta's porch and I heard her on the phone saying, "J.W., I just can't do that! You're going to have to quit asking me! I'm going to have to tell Louise if you don't!" I walked in and Loretta's face turned red. "Loretta, is J.W. bothering you?" "He wants to go with me, Louise! When I go down the road to see my mother every afternoon, he is parked down there at the end with his car across the road and won't let me pass. He stands there and begs me to meet him and go out with him. I said, 'J.W., why would you want to go out

with me . . . I'm pregnant!' Louise, I've been wanting to tell you for a long time but I didn't know how to approach you . . . I wanted to keep you as my friend. He wants me to write him letters at his post office box downtown. I told him I wouldn't do it."

After that, we stopped seeing Loretta and Verle like we had. One day I saw Loretta in the yard and we got to talking about something, the weather or the kids, and she said, "I'm sorry, Louise, that we can't be good friends like we were, but you understand why, it's because of how J.W. is." I could never have friends.

WHEN I WAS ELEVEN AND JUST BEGINNING TO FEEL A HEATED ATTRACTION *to the opposite sex, my mother asked Mama Lee to take on the task of telling me the facts of life. This was prompted by my best friend's new brassiere, which Daleanne made sure everybody knew about—either her bra strap was hanging down or she was raising her arms so we could all gape through the open holes of her sleeveless blouse. We had been eating sassafras leaves, because when we asked our sixteen-year-old neighbor how she got so big on top, she said the sassafras did it.*

*One summer morning when she was visiting from Louisiana, Mama Lee walked into my bedroom with my mother in close tow. I opened my eyes to her smell of fresh bath and talcum powder. My grandmother was wearing navy blue silk pajamas with thin white piping running all around the edges. A slender tube of nitroglycerin for her heart condition was held in place with a tiny white satin ribbon. Her fingernails were carefully polished in American Beauty red, and matching lipstick was already in place at this early hour. My grandmother had an air of being somebody important. She lay down beside me, placing her arm around my shoulder. My mother sat on the edge of the bed with a dish towel in one hand and a plate in the other, as if she had been caught midstream in the drying of breakfast dishes.*

*"Patricia, you're eleven years old now and it's time you understood about becoming a woman," Mama Lee began. "You know, the Bible tells us that Eve was the first woman created by God, and Adam was the first man. They were husband and wife. They were our first parents." She smiled and pulled me a little closer to her. I heard her voice distantly — "God created the Garden of Eden for them to live near Him in heaven." I was thinking about Robert Beecher, who lived up on the hill, and about the letter I had found in the yard. "A snake that was really the devil tempted Eve to eat of the tree of good and evil which God had forbidden." In the letter, Robert said that he thought about me at night when he went to sleep and that he really liked me. The ink was all blurred from days of dampness, so I couldn't make out much else. "Eve ate of the fruit and gave some to Adam. When God found out, He cast them out of Eden into the world." I could see Robert walking up and down the road; I knew he was hoping to catch sight of me. "Adam and Eve committed the first sin. God punishes those who disobey Him. God said Adam would have to forever toil by the sweat of his brow to bring forth food from the earth and Eve would have to endure the pain of labor to bring forth children onto the earth." I wondered if Robert would kiss me like he said he would, like they did*

*it in the movies. Mama Lee read to me from my Bible, the white leather one with "Patricia Ann Clarkson" embossed in gold on the cover. I was a descendent of Eve, all women were, my grandmother told me. "All women after Eve must bear Eve's burden," she said. "When you are about twelve or thirteen you will bleed and that means you are ready to be a woman. When you get older and get married you will bear children." My mother, sitting silently, furrowed her brow and began crying, saying, "Patricia, I can't believe you are growing up so fast like this." My grandmother held one hand above her waist and one hand below it. "Until you are married, Patricia, you must never, never let any boy touch your private parts." Her hands still in position, Mama Lee illustrated by patting the "parts."*

## HIGHER GROUND

After your father lost his job in St. Louis, he could not find a good steady job. If it hadn't been for our savings, I don't know what in the world would have happened to us in those days. We were getting pretty desperate, so your daddy said he knew cars were selling good in Greenfield and he went down and asked Don Woodson, a friend of our family, for a job. So your father stood out there on the lot and tried to sell cars. I'd never seen him get down so low about anything in all my life. He said he thought he was getting too old for anything anymore and if I'm not mistaken he was just forty years old. I had never seen a man stand in front of a mirror as much as him. He was always worried to death about every little pimple or gray hair.

One day he said that there just wasn't nothing left in Greenfield for us. He told me Norma was pressing him again and that the only way to get away from her was to leave town. He said, "Louise, are you willing to go with me and move down south where Mother is?" He convinced me that he was truly trying to get away from Norma. So he called his mother long distance, down to Kemper, to see if she could help and she said, "Yes, come on down! By the time you get down here I'll have you a job." Jackie Lee said we could stay with her until we could find a place. I hated to leave where I had lived all of my life, but I thought that if you were married to somebody and they don't have a job, there's nothing you can do but try to help him, try to make it.

We had used up all our savings, so J. W. decided to sell the house we still owned on Clover Street. He never told me but I think he got a good price for it. That was the end of our home.

I guess it took a month to get everything together. We had to sell a lot of our furniture. We gave so many nice things away because we didn't have room to take them with us — all the porch furniture and our yard swing and my mother's big old antique dining room table and chairs. Everything I had canned that summer I gave to Loretta next door.

We had to take you all out of school. It was very, very sad. You didn't want to leave school and all your teachers and friends. It was bad the way we had to do it. J. W. wouldn't let you all tell your school or friends that we was leaving. He said he just wanted to slip out of town. Wiley didn't say much, he was young, but you stomped your feet and cried and begged me for us not to go. I tried to explain to you that there wasn't nothing I could do, we just had to make a change, and I know you cried and cried about leaving. Your daddy never had to hear any of this, 'cause you all were afraid of him. I felt so bad, but I knew we had to go to higher ground. That's all there was to it. We had to go.

The last night Loretta and Verle cooked a big supper for us, fresh corn and tomatoes from the garden and catfish Verle caught up at Kentucky Lake. Daleanne came over so she could say goodbye to you. I called my good friend Peggy, who had been my neighbor over on Clover Street, to tell her goodbye. She was my very best friend. We both cried on the telephone because we knew we'd never see each other again.

We were on our way to Louisiana, "God's country," that's what J.W. called it. We took our black cocker spaniel, Skipper, with us. We left about midnight and you all slept in the back of the car with Skipper. We took a lot of things to eat and we were all happy, talking about how things were going to be when we got there. Your father said he would take whatever job he could get. I felt like this was a new beginning for us. We were all together.

LAKE PONTCHARTRAIN CAUSEWAY · NEW ORLEANS · 1992

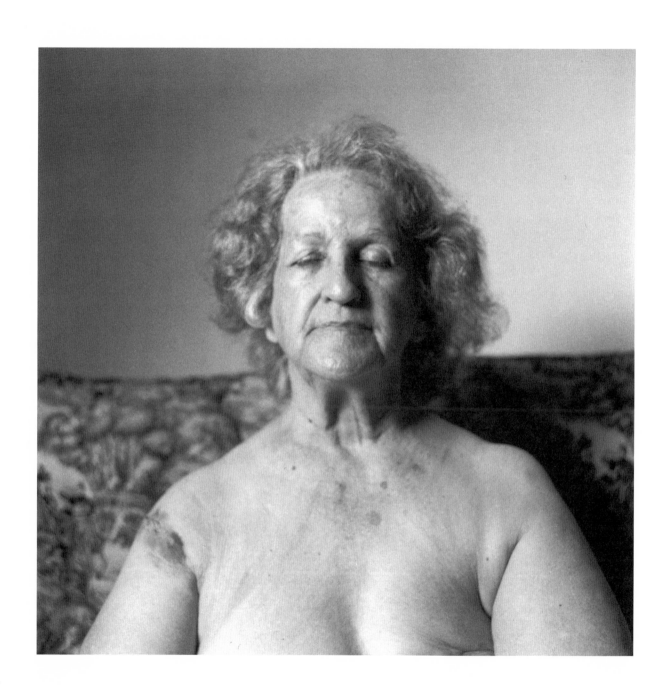

LOUISE AFTER HER MASTECTOMY, 1994

# 3

# A DOUBLE LIFE

# THIRD INTERVIEW
## August 11, 1993

*It was unbearably hot in Texas. Mother was living in darkness, her curtains perpetually drawn to stave off the burning sunlight. I was sleeping on the living room couch, which had been reupholstered in an English hunt scene. The array of mismatched furniture, rug, and curtains reminded me of our home thirty years earlier in New Orleans. I lay awake and scanned the room, feeling the old fear of being trapped in the web of my family. In the morning, Mother turned to face me, suds dripping off the rubber gloves she was wearing because I demanded that she protect her sore and cracked hands. I sat in the doorway of the kitchen with a tape recorder held at arm's length. She told me of her compassion for my father, explaining that she would not let anyone suffer, that she would crawl through snow up to her hips to help anyone in need. Why did she stay with him all those years? I had asked this question many times before, but I kept asking, because I could not accept the answer. I was embarrassed by my denial of the truth, knowing how destructive delusions could be. My energy was drained — I had been here too long this time. I would photograph Mother that day. I am a photographer. I needed to hold on to who I am.*

# A BUSINESS TRIP

I remember when we arrived in Kemper, Jackie Lee acted like she wasn't very friendly. I felt like she thought she was taking on something she didn't really want to do, like we were coming in on her privacy. It made me feel real bad. J.W. even noticed it himself.

It wasn't long before it was Christmas time. Right then I found out your father had talked to his mother and told her that he had to go back to Greenfield on business. He was always going on a trip or telling me he's going on a trip! J.W. asked her, "Would it be all right if Louise and the kids stay here in the house with you until I can get back?" She told him, "No, they cannot stay here. I'm leaving myself to go to Birmingham to spend Christmas with my sister Enid. Why do you, a father, have to go off and leave your kids at Christmas and go back to Greenfield? Your wife and children cannot stay here while you go off chasing some woman!"

I said to your grandmother, "Jackie Lee, I wish I could stay here and we could all have Christmas together . . ." She said, "Well, I can't do anything because I've got my plans made and Enid's expecting me and I'm not going to stay home to please J.W." There was nothing I could do, Patricia, your father was his own boss. He said, "You'll have to find some place to go." I was very depressed! We weren't gonna have no Christmas. I didn't know what to do so I called your great grandmother, Big Mama, and asked her if we could come and visit for Christmas.

Your father didn't say nothing about Christmas presents for you all, so I asked him, "What are you going to buy the children this year?"

"Well, I don't have any money."

"We have to buy them something!"

"I'm sure your grandmother and my mother will see to it that they have a good Christmas." That year J. W. did not buy one present for us. He had to go on his trip . . . that's where he spent his money.

Your daddy drove us to Memphis and let us out. Big Mama tried to do the best she could for us. I told you all your daddy was going to Greenfield on business. You all was happy to know that we could go see Big Mama, 'cause you all loved Big Mama. You all never complained. I don't know what I would have done if the Lord didn't give me such good children! It was so heartbreaking the way Big Mama was living. She was alone. She was almost blind. She didn't have very much at all but she did have presents for y'all. I told her I wanted her to come down and stay with me but I was having trouble with J. W. and I didn't know how much longer I was gonna be with him. She was very upset . . . I know it sure was a very sad Christmas for me.

When your daddy came back to get us, it was five o'clock in the morning. It was so bad because you all were asleep and I had to pick your brother up in my arms and lay him in the car. We drove in the car all day long and late that afternoon we were in front of Jackie Lee's house.

I lived in fear for what was coming next. Our furniture was still in storage and we didn't have much and your daddy kept saying we couldn't afford the kind of house we needed for our furniture. We wasn't back from Memphis three weeks and early one morning a telegram came for J. W. I read it. It said, "I will see you in three days. Norma." I was so stunned, I couldn't move. J. W. brought me to Louisiana and then he brought Norma. He said she was following him. He said he didn't know what to do.

I didn't know how much sadder I could get, then one morning Jackie Lee said, "Louise, I have something to tell you. A friend of mine happened to see J. W. over in Slidell — she saw him moving furniture into a house. I took it upon myself to call that place where you all have your furniture stored and they told me Mr. Clarkson came over there two days ago and moved all his stuff out of storage." Your grandmother got a friend to take us there to the address and she and I walked up to the door and knocked on it. When nobody came, we walked around to the back and peeped through the window and there was my mother's nightstand and my dresser! We went home and waited for J.W. "You gave all my furniture away! It's not over! She's...here!" He said, "Don't say that...I'm still with you... Norma came down here for a couple of days and didn't have no place to stay and I had to *loan* her our furniture." I cried to think I didn't have nothing anymore. We had sold our house. We had used up our savings. He didn't have a good steady job—I couldn't leave him now. He leaned over and put his hands on me and kissed me and said, "Oh, come on. Perk up. Trust in God. We'll work this thing out someway." He'd just try to give me some little encouragement to hold on a little bit longer. That's all I been doin' all my life is claspin' my hands and holdin' onto the mountain side.

Jackie Lee told your father we had to leave her house. She said she was through helping him. She told him, "You've lied to everybody, J.W. Have you lied to yourself, too?"

DRIVING SOUTH I FELT MYSELF GROWING IN AWARENESS AS THE PINES *became taller and taller. By the time we were on Louisiana soil, my parents had most tragically fallen from grace. We were in God's country, my father kept joyfully announcing, but to me it might as well have been Mars. The air was thick and moist. Spanish moss, gray and tangled, dripped from immense white oaks that lined the avenues and shaded the backyards. Kudzu vine grew everywhere, twisting and winding itself around most anything. Fans stirred the air as we sat about in our cotton dresses, humidity frizzing our hair till a comb wouldn't go through it. My teeth ached from so much pecan pie. The grown-ups drank cup after cup of the thick syrup my grandmother called coffee. I couldn't seem to get enough sleep and thought I must have the sleeping sickness, but really I was just homesick, fifteen hours south of where I wanted to be.*

*We lived like Gypsies in my grandmother's small, four-room home where she worked long hours making fancy dresses for the wealthy class of St. Clement Parish. With all the fine clothes needed for weddings, debutante balls, homecomings, and holidays, Mama Lee was always up to her eyeballs in tulle and taffeta. Her gentleman caller was a Mr. Rawling, a mortician at Schoen's Funeral Home, from a "very old and fine Kemper family." He was a man of leviathan proportions, and his kindness matched his size. His car, a long black Lincoln, impressed us all. I slept on the pull-out sofa bed, Wiley on the recliner in Mama Lee's workroom, Mother and Daddy in the back storage room. Our days were tenuous. My brother and I walked to parochial school in our uniforms each day, wondering where we would be living when we returned home. Our father slept days and worked nights on a job building Lake Pontchartrain Causeway, a twenty-three-mile-long bridge that would link Kemper on the north shore with New Orleans.*

*I mourned and grieved for all that I had left behind in Kentucky. I felt nothing could ever be the same again. Angry and turning inward with depression, I became*

*dull in spirit and ragged in appearance. I was criticized for being ingrown and un-
cooperative. I overheard Mama Lee telling her best friend, Bessie, what a shame it
was that Patricia was "without personality." Wiley, on the other hand, was a "bub-
bly, cheerful, child," she said, sounding relieved that one of us had turned out the
way she had hoped. High-minded, I never tried to prove her wrong.*

*One day snooping in my father's briefcase, I found a rough sketch of a letter in
his handwriting. It told of J.W.'s marriage to Norma the day after Christmas. It
had been part of his plan when he left Kentucky. He said Norma didn't return
with him to Louisiana, because she had wanted to wait until her daughter's school
year was completed. I was stung by his words of betrayal and the memory of being
forced to leave my home in the middle of my school year. Still, the hurt I felt was
not greater than the need to protect my parents. I decided not to tell anyone about
the secret marriage of J.W. to Norma.*

*From the age of twelve I was on my own. Looking at my parents, I thought an
absentminded God had placed them side by side. Because I had heard my father
question my mother's abilities so many times, I had come to believe that she wasn't
capable. I sensed that my mother felt herself to be as much a child as I was. One
day I passed a woman on the street pushing her baby in a stroller and felt an urge to
rescue the baby, thinking, "That mother cannot take care of that baby!" A moment
later, I knew that the baby I wanted to rescue was myself. We had come to accept my
father's absence as normal, but when I saw that Mother was afraid to make deci-*

*sions and had no power to help us, I began to have a recurrent nightmare in which a staggering giant was holding a globe above his head and I was on it, struggling to stand upright and keep from falling off. The fear of not being able to stand upright stayed with me long after I awoke.*

*As the months passed, our possessions, stored in the Safe Stop Storage warehouse, took on a patina of mold. My father shook his head, lamenting the scarcity of "proper" housing. Our grandmother was very edgy with us constantly underfoot, which caused Mother to be overly apologetic and embarrassed. Wiley stayed spellbound by Mama Lee's twenty-four-inch Sylvania television. My bottom lip had grown at least an inch since we had arrived. I hated everything, and I vented my anger on Wiley. If he as much touched anything that belonged to me, my fists would turn into hammers, pounding into his back until he had fallen to his knees in submission. We all passed down our pain; Wiley would later do the same thing to our little brother, Davy, soon to be born. It was like the pecking order of the chickens on Mimosa Hill, where the bigger ones attacked the one that was smaller and less able. They pecked and pecked on a Rhode Island Red we had named Henry, until his head was bald and bleeding. Mother, with her compassionate nature, saved Henry, allowing him to live like a prince on our back porch until he got fat enough to be killed and eaten. I realized that life was unjust, but I had decided I was not going to be trampled on like my mother, who shook her head in resignation and told me, "Life just ain't no fair...it just ain't no fair at all."*

WE MOVED FROM MAMA LEE'S TO A DILAPIDATED AND SHABBY FURNISHED *house on a busy corner across from the A&P. Daddy set up a darkroom and Mother set up an ironing room. My father promised us that it was only temporary, and asked that we be patient while he looked for a more appropriate home. On the day of our move, we inquired, "Mother, where's Skipper?" "Your daddy had to give Skipper away...to a colored family," Mother explained, saying she was sorry but she couldn't make him change his mind. Dogs weren't allowed in furnished houses. I was furious. Wiley began crying, "Oh Mama, where's Skipper, where's Skipper...?" I threw all my mother's clean folded clothes that she was unpacking on the floor and then slammed out of the house, running down the street, hoping I could go so hard and fast that my body would rip to pieces and fly off in all directions. As I ran, I had a sense of becoming free. When I stopped, I was in front of Mama Lee's house.*

*My grandmother was outside leaning into a car window talking with a customer. Filled with mourning and exhaustion, barefooted, I wished I could do a magic act of disappearance and reappearance as another girl, a girl just back from playing a round of tennis, all dressed in court whites, glowing in my suntan and youthfulness. Mama Lee was smiling and posturing in her proud officious manner; I could see my father in that gesture. Turning her body flat in my direction, she said, "Oh, here's my granddaughter, Patricia!" I knew I was expected to walk over and be so very charming and smart, like a graduate of Miss So-and-So's finishing school.*

*Everybody in Kemper knew my grandmother. Folks would say, "You're the grand-daughter of Jackie Lee Harris . . . how nice!" The ladies in the neighborhood were jealous of Mrs. Harris, I had heard, clucking that she was "too independent, making her own money and owning two homes."*

*Mama Lee boasted of having a "good background." I saw her polished manners and social etiquette. I defied her and protected myself from the feelings I had of being nothing. I didn't tell my grandmother how I wanted to die, how I felt nothing but anger and hatred for the people on whom I depended. She didn't ask me what was wrong. I guess she thought I was just a sullen and ugly child. There wasn't anybody to whom I could tell my feelings. Oh, how we missed Skipper, but there was no bringing Skipper back.*

*I made friends at my new school, rich girls mostly, and slowly forgot about my sorrows. Like my father and his mother, I had a knack for pretending to be more than I was. Somehow I was able to keep up with friends who had their own horses and swimming pools. For spending money, after school I weeded and tended Mama Lee's flower garden — she won awards for her petunias. A flower bed and many window boxes kept me busy until dusk. Afterwards my grandmother and I sat eating big bowls of chocolate swirl ice cream while watching Perry Como, Loretta Young, or Liberace. She absolutely adored Liberace, and nobody dared refer to him as a "fruit," which is what gay men were sometimes called.*

*One afternoon just as I was finishing up with the gardening, Mama Lee came and sat on the low brick wall that edged the petunias. Not smiling as she usually was, she told me that a customer had just left her with a bit of gossip. The girls at school said I smelled bad, like I had peed on myself. She asked me if I was having problems controlling my bladder. Her eyes were boring a hole into me; I didn't know what to tell her. I felt smaller and smaller, unworthy even to touch the weeds in her garden. I knew she wouldn't understand if I said that the problem was my nerves, and that to fix it I would have to fix my parents, and I didn't think anybody could do that.*

## "MY REAL WIFE"

When the bridge job run out, your daddy got a job working for an insurance company in New Orleans. So we moved fifty miles from Kemper and rented a duplex house in New Orleans. A couple of months after we had been living in there, J.W. came home and said his boss and his wife was having a fiftieth wedding anniversary party and they asked J.W. to come and to bring his wife. I dressed up and I went with him. I remember when I was there, I felt like J.W.'s boss's wife kept looking at me with a puzzled look on her face. I could catch her eye on me. I thought, "Do I look all right? Is anything wrong?" I was self-conscious because I wasn't used to going out and meeting people and being around people. I told J.W. later and he said, "It's just your imagination. There wasn't nothing wrong. You looked nice." Anyway, I remember it was a nice party and we had a good time, but I knew something was wrong. I felt it.

On Monday morning, J.W. went to work and his boss called him into his office and he said, "I'm sorry to have to ask you this, John, but are you having any trouble with your marriage?"

J.W. said, "No . . . I'm not."

His boss asked him, "What is your wife's name?"

Your daddy said, "Louise . . . why?"

His boss said, "Something strange happened and I thought I should tell you about it. I've had a woman to call me up on the phone and say that she was your wife and that the woman that you are living with is not your wife at all—that you are living with your ex-wife."

J.W. said, "Louise is my real wife. We've been married for eighteen years—we have two children. I used to be involved with this woman but I'm married to Louise. Louise is my real wife."

Your daddy came home and told me what had happened. He said Norma was living in New Orleans, and he was really worried because he was afraid she might make him lose his job again. He said that we might have to move back to Kemper. I said, "Oh, Lord, J.W., I hope not—this is awful, taking the kids in and out of school. They don't like it and I don't like it!"

Oh, well, Patricia, I know that you're sick and tired of hearing about all of this. My life was becoming a terrible pattern that never seemed to ever end. I must of lost my pride. I must of lost my self-esteem. I got so I just let your father walk all over on me and let him walk on top of my face and I took it. I know this makes me look like a fool. You don't understand me. I don't understand me. I was just living on a dream all the time, with him promising me and begging me and telling me he loved me, that he would never leave me. I felt if he did go off and leave me I couldn't make it in the world because I didn't know how to go out to get a job. I didn't know how to take care of myself. I didn't know much of anything. I didn't know how to fight for my rights. I was like a child because your father never did give me any privilege of having money for me to go out and pay bills. I never had the privilege to do anything. He run the house. He run the children. He run everything. I was like a maid that stayed inside the house and listened to everything he said, and everything he said I believed.

AT SOPHIE B. WRIGHT JUNIOR HIGH, IN THE IRISH CHANNEL SCHOOL *district of New Orleans, I learned about gangs, knives, sex, drinking, and buying cigarettes for a nickel. The school was run by a gang called the River Rats. The girls' chapter was led by a toughie named Linda Morino. These girls could decide that they didn't like another girl for many reasons, one being that she wore falsies. When this was suspected, a spy was sent to each girl's stall during gym class and, if any foam rubber was discovered pinned to someone's bra, after school they would jump her, strip her, and hang her bra on the tree outside the school entrance.*

*My father kept me under constant surveillance. He drove me to and from school and harped endlessly on the subject of boys. I was a bit physically overdeveloped for my age, and boys were attracted to me. I defied my father, matching him in talk and argument. He punished me with confinement. But I was not afraid of him — I felt he had no power over me. At night I put pillows in my bed, turned on the radio, and slipped out the back door. Mother knew what I was doing — she was an accomplice.*

*"Boys only want one thing!" he would instruct loudly. I couldn't invite boys home; my father would scare them half to death with his interrogations. I wasn't*

55-56
ST. PETER

PATRICIA, AGE TWELVE, 1955–56

*allowed to date, but I did make out with boys in the back seats of their cars. I deliberately wanted to be a bad girl. Boys asked good girls to be their girlfriends and then made out with the bad girls. Boys wanted good girls to marry. I didn't want a boyfriend, nor did I want to get married.*

*My first potential real date was with Rudy D'Angelo, a cute greaser who owned his own car. He asked me to be his eighth grade prom date. At first I was excited, but then I wondered if there was any point in even asking my father if I could go. I knew what he would say: "What kind of name is D'Angelo? Where does his family live? What does his father do? You're too young to go out with a boy." My mother, who sometimes knew how to catch my father when he was feeling like he owed her a favor, told me she had been working on him and prodded me to go in and ask. By some miracle, he agreed to let me go to the prom with Rudy, but said he would have to drive us there and pick us up. I ran out with my good news, beaming with joy, hugging and kissing and jumping around my mother. My grandmother, Mama Lee, made me a beautiful strapless white satin dress with a blue bow, a bit too grand for a Sophie B. Wright junior high prom, but I was going; that was the important thing.*

*The night of the prom, my mother said, "Before you get dressed, go in and remind your father that he has to drive you all." Hesitating at the doorway of my father's disheveled quarters, I was hit by the smell of stale cigarette smoke. Daddy's large frame sinking deep down into those rumpled sheets and his fixed stare made me think of a dead man in a casket. He didn't look up as I approached him. He said he didn't remember anything about a prom, and when I began tearfully and loudly protesting, he said he didn't want to hear another word about it. I stormed out of the house, slamming the door behind me. Hot with rage outside in the night air, I ran as fast as I could to the home of my best friend, Juliana. She had five brothers and sisters, and her mother was remarried to a young, blond air force captain. There was a creative feeling in Juliana's home. The casual, spacious rooms were full of books and records but held little furniture; plush European rugs were comfortably littered with toys, clothes, and cats. Long gauzy curtains flowed at open French doors, and assorted children loafed on a big sofa, eating a pizza as they watched TV. I flopped my body down next to my friend's and grabbed a piece of pizza. Juliana's mother, Ada, who could have doubled for Rita Hayworth, announced, "Come on, girls, go get dressed and let's cruise down Bourbon."*

*We put on black velvet Capri pants and scarves from Ada's closet, and applied limitless amounts of orange lipstick, black eyeliner, and green eye shadow. As we piled into Ada's '57 Chevy convertible, I thought of Rudy and his predicament but forgot about him as soon as we crossed Canal and started down Bourbon. The three of us, squeezed together in the front seat, gawked at nightclub strippers wearing G-strings and pasties. When Ada winked and smiled, we got the royal treatment — barkers at burlesque clubs held doors wide open, inviting us in for free.*

I WAS CONFUSED ABOUT WHAT CLASS MY FAMILY BELONGED TO NOW. IN *Louisiana our middle-class facade had begun to crumble. There was always some incongruous or missing element: a house without furniture; a nice dress but not the proper shoes; a father who dressed and acted like a cultured gentleman in public but was a raving maniac at home; a two-parent family in which the father was married to somebody else; a mother who said "ain't" but a grandmother who dressed her grandchildren in designer clothes and expected the "king's English" in return.*

*As I became a woman, my father made me the object of his jokes. One day, wearing pressed and creased red shorts and a starched white blouse with its collar turned up, I was leaving the house and had to pass through the living room, where he sat slumped in a chair. I strode by him with confidence. He began laughing, "Just who do you think you are? You look like nothing but a whore!" I can still hear his roaring laughter. It seemed as though the more I tried to look good and do well, the harder he pressed down on me. I didn't know why he wanted to break me, but I was determined to resist and hold tight to my beliefs. When I needed my first bra, I stole the money from him because I was afraid he would make fun of me for thinking that I was big enough to wear one. After school, red-faced with embarrassment, I bought the bra, and, although the storekeeper didn't ask, I explained that it was for my mother. When I got home and saw J.W.'s car out front, I hid the package under the porch steps. Later that night, after he had left, I retrieved it.*

*At the beginning of each school year my father continued his practice of buying all my school clothes from the Montgomery Ward catalog: four skirts and four blouses, a cardigan sweater set, a pair of black flats and a pair of black-and-white oxfords. When I complained, I was reminded that the door was open, and that, in fact, he was looking forward to the day when I would be eighteen and his job would be over. He was doing his duty and no more. From the catalog clothes I created what I thought were stylish outfits. I made tucks at the waistline of a plain blouse, giving it some shape, and altered a pleated skirt into a straight one. I took a razor blade to the black flats, cutting them low so that the cracks of my toes would show, and once I even sprayed some dye on them so I could have red shoes.*

*After a teacher was kind enough to tell me that I was "inappropriately dressed," I gave up on catalog clothes and tried to wear what Mama Lee made for me. I looked like a thief from Laura Ashley, wearing my grandmother's debutante fashions without the right shoes or accessories, which she didn't supply. What I really needed to fit in at Wright was a leather jacket and motorcycle boots. A new friend, Sylvie Van, saved my life. She loved my nice-girl clothes and didn't mind switching with me in the girls' bathroom every morning before the bell rang. Her tight black skirt, tight pink sweater, and black flats looked good, I thought—and a cigarette really finished off my new look. When the last bell of the school day rang, dismissing all the hoodlums, Sylvie and I would do our morning ritual in reverse. Returning to the self my father expected, I would run out through the* school's double doors and try to slither unseen into J.W.'s still-alive 1949 green Dodge with its Kentucky plates.

My father had a decent job with an office, an expense account, a secretary, and a company car, but he sometimes didn't even have a dime to give me for milk to drink with the sandwich Mother had made. Most kids went to K&B's, a drugstore, for Cokes and burgers. I would eat my sandwich behind the locked door of a stall in the girls' bathroom, then join my friends at K&B's, just getting a Coke and saying I wasn't hungry. In a few years Wiley would throw his brown bag lunch in the trash right outside the kitchen door, causing Mother to worry that he wasn't eating and making her feel more helpless than ever because she didn't have the money to give him. She would cry and apologize to us for not being able to help more with our problems.

At fifteen, I started looking for work. One day, having taken a long bus ride, I went into a place called the Escape to apply for a babysitting job. A hand waved me towards the back, and I walked through a dark bar stinking from years of spilled cocktails and cigarette smoke. In the office, I looked down at a baby about eight months old crawling around in a playpen. Standing above my potential charge, the father said, "Yeah, this baby needs a sitter"; then, hesitating, he said that with my looks I could make a lot more money. "Oh, yeah?" I said, surprised and sensing that there was something wrong with this guy, who said his name was Floyd. He said, "Sure, we need a looker like you around the bar." Floyd made it *sound easy. All I had to do was sit at the bar and let men buy me a drink. When I told him I wasn't old enough to drink, he laughed and said, "Oh, yeah! That's no problem." He told me that for just sitting at the bar I could make fifty dollars a week. He was pushy, but I thought it sounded good, so I agreed. He said that Patricia was too hard to remember, and that I would be called Patty.*

*The day I went there to start, I was so scared that I went in as if I were looking for somebody and then walked quickly out. The bar was mostly empty, so I forced myself to go back. I slipped onto a bar stool, and a middle-aged man in a sharkskin suit sat down next to me, saying, "Whadya drinking — how about another?" I said, "Okay." When the barmaid brought it, the man turned around to look at me. I said, "Excuse me," and headed for the door.*

*I later learned that Floyd had hired me to be a "B" (bar) girl, which was against the law. Bar owners would use young girls to lure and deceive lonely men, who would keep paying for vodka martinis while the "B" girl drank water. I had wanted to become Patty — I didn't know how else to make money. But I was held back by the shame I felt in the presence of the middle-aged man, who reminded me of my father.*

When I came to visit you all in New Orleans, J.W. could not keep his hands off me. He was always rubbing and patting me. I think he was looking for sex. On the day I left to go back to Greenfield, he wanted to take me to the train station and he wanted Louise to stay home. When he did that I knew what he had in mind and I knew Louise knew, too. He asked me if I wanted to spend a night with him. He said, "Loretta, you could stay one more night and nobody would know. We could go out on the town and have a good time..." I wouldn't do it! The next time I talked to your mother, always in the back of her mind, she thought that I did spend that night with J.W., but as God is my witness, I didn't do it. He said there was no way we could get caught. I said, "No! You can't seem to get it through your head, I just really don't want to." It was just too sickening for me. He said, "You're missing a good time...I don't think you've ever had a real man before." In other words, he was going to teach me something that I'd never done before. I wasn't used to a person that sure of himself. I thought it gave him a thrill to shock me like that. When Verle and I came to visit you all in New Orleans we all went out dancing. We partied. We'd eat out. We had a good time together. Louise could laugh and joke and be happy. She didn't sit around and dwell on her problems. I said to him, "Now, J.W., you have a wife and you have a girlfriend so what do you want with me?" He said, "Well, I really don't know what I want in life." I thought your father was a mixed-up man. Your mother was probably the right one for your father, he just didn't know it. I thought he was after the conquest and the only way to keep J.W. would be to keep the conquest going.

*Loretta*
*Greenfield, Kentucky*

J.W., POSING FOR PATRICIA, BOGUE FALAYA RIVER PARK, KEMPER, LOUISIANA, C. 1955–57

LOUISE IN MATERNITY DRESS AT LAKE PONTCHARTRAIN, C. 1958

# A TRAP

One night J.W. was out late and when he came home he had intercourse with me while I was sleeping. J.W. knew exactly what he was doing. He took me when I was half asleep so I couldn't protect myself. It felt like it was a trap that he had put me in. I was forty years old.

When the doctor told me, I was very, very upset. I started crying, and I said, "I'm too old to have a child!" I was thinking, "All these things I had to go through, I have to go through again." The doctor said, "Honey, if you can get pregnant, you're not too old! I think you're lucky to have a child at forty years old!" When I told J.W. I was pregnant, he laughed, he actually laughed! He was tickled to death. I told him, "I don't need any more kids." He said, "Well, did you think you were just gonna have two kids—you're gonna have a lot of kids before it's over with."

There is something I didn't tell you, Patricia, because I am so embarrassed about it... one of the reasons I was so upset about being pregnant was that before your daddy and I left Greenfield, I signed the papers for your father to get another divorce. You know how your father is, Patricia... I couldn't ever say no to him. It was odd the way it happened. Somebody I knew called me one day and said, "I see in the paper where you and J.W. are getting a divorce." I laughed and said, "That can't be nothing but a gag!," but my heart skipped a beat, because I knew it might be true.

When I asked your father, he said Norma was on him again—he said he just needed to get a divorce "to make a point." He had already filed—he brought in the papers and asked me to agree. He said, "If you agree then we'll go on as we are and I promise you we'll get remarried again right away like we did before. If you don't I'm afraid she's going to cause us more trouble." I remember I got very upset and cried, and he said, "Come on, Louise, I'll take you out to dinner and we'll talk." Your father poured his heart out to me. "I love you, I will never give you up, Louise, I will always love you." I said, "If you love me, I don't understand why you'd want a divorce." He said, "I don't understand myself . . . I just need to get these papers so I can show her I can get a divorce — she threatened me and told me she knew I couldn't do it — I need to show her." I remember him begging me that day. He put his arms around me, he told me how much he loved me . . . trying to kiss me, trying to love me . . . I said I felt strange not being married and he just said, "Don't you tell nobody and I won't tell nobody. Between us and God we're still married."

It was a quiet divorce . . . I just signed the papers. Nothing changed. We stayed together. I was like a child. He would tell me to do something and I would do it. You children never seemed to understand — I was trapped!

I tried to hide my pregnancy — I didn't want anybody to know. My grandmother, Big Mama, was sick and had come down from Memphis to live with us, and I guess J. W. let her because she paid him with her pension check. I especially didn't want her to know I was pregnant. I kept it from her for a long time and then I had to start wearing those dresses. When she found out she got very mad! I remember her knocking her cane against the table and saying, "There's nothing lower than that snake in the grass J. W. Clarkson, Jr."

Before long your father had moved us back across Lake Pontchartrain . . . way out in the country. When I saw the house he got for us I cried. It was a chicken coop, that's what I call it. Every day after I found out I was pregnant I kept pleading with him, "When are we gonna go down and get remarried?" He would say, "Just as soon as I can get up on my feet." I couldn't talk to nobody about it—Jackie Lee didn't know, my mother didn't know—you kids sure didn't know! But, Patricia, there's something else in the story that I have never told you, that I didn't really want anybody to know. Remember that time we went to Big Mama's for Christmas and your daddy left us there for three days? Your father went up to Greenfield and married Norma. He had to break down and tell me that he had married her and he was having a hard time trying to get a divorce from her. That's the reason he kept on telling me no when I was begging for us to go get married again.

I didn't think things could get any worse. Then late one afternoon your father came in from New Orleans and asked me to make him a fresh pot of coffee, that he had something he wanted to talk to me about.

"Louise, I know when I tell you, you're probably going to get mad, and in fact if you feel like you need to leave me, I'll understand."

I said, "Oh, my God, J.W., what have you done now?"

"Louise . . . Norma had a baby."

"When on God's earth did this happen . . . ?"

"About a year ago."

I slammed his coffee cup down so hard on the table it broke and the hot coffee poured all over his good suit pants. I was eight months pregnant . . . I told J.W., "Oh, I know what you have done—the night she had her baby, that's when you came back and got me pregnant, that's when it happened!"

He just said, "Whatever you want to do, I'll understand."

"Just what do you think I could do when I'm nearly eight months pregnant! Where do you think I would go? No, I'm not leaving you at all! I think you've done me a terrible injustice! I'm going to stay right here and you're going to take care of my baby!"

He put his arm around me and he said, "I'm so sorry for everything that's happened—I've gotten myself in a terrible mess, but with your help we can get free of it. I love you and I'll be right there with you when the baby is born."

"J.W., I don't understand why you cannot really get away from this woman!"

"It's on my mind all the time. I'm going to do something about it, I promise you."

I know one thing, Patricia, everything your father did to me he did to Norma, too.

WE SEEMED TO BE IN HIDING, AS IF WE WERE OUTCASTS FROM THE NORMAL world. Daddy had moved us to Abita Springs, a small hamlet outside Kemper. Wiley and I got to school by bus each morning. Kemper High was the fourth school I had attended since we had arrived in Louisiana two and a half years earlier. "Out in the sticks!" is how Big Mama described our new home. Way back off the main road and overwhelmed by lush vegetation, it was a tin-roofed cabin with a screened-in porch. When a car appeared on our dead-end road, it was usually somebody lost. My father drove to work in New Orleans every morning at dawn. He didn't always come home in the evening, but on Fridays, right before dark, I could hear his tires pressing into the gravel, a sound that would forever after remind me of him. In a minute or two he would be standing among us, like a visitor, grinning and smelling of bourbon.

Every night when I went to sleep I got into a car and began a journey. I drove *across an endless bridge with no shore in sight or destination in mind. I balanced my vehicle on a narrow band of road in the darkest night above treacherous cold waters. Unable to stop or to go back, I could only go forward towards an invisible shore, which I never reached. In my waking life, I looked around and felt ashamed of our home, of my mother, my father and myself. I hoped none of the new friends I was making would ever try to visit me. The girls I met at Kemper High weren't gang members but girls who had maids to make their beds, swimming pools in their back yards, and horses in their pastures. Most took some kind of lessons, piano or dance. I spent time at their homes, but I couldn't swim or ride a horse or play an instrument. In fact, I had no social graces or instruction on how to do anything. I often wondered why they liked me.*

*Wiley didn't know how to swim either, since we had never been allowed to go near water. Anything my brother and I had ever wanted to do was forbidden by our father. Back in Greenfield, on Halloween, Wiley and I used to watch from the window as kids trick-or-treated up and down our block. When I begged to learn to play the piano, my father responded, "Oh, Patricia, why do you want to do that, you have so many other things to do..." Wiley was asked to join Little League, but Daddy said it was too dangerous. Mother took me to try out for a movie they were making in our town about the Lindbergh baby kidnapping, and I was picked. Our father saw no reason why we should do any of these things. "I'll think about it" is all we ever heard from him.*

*On Abita Road, the enchantment of nature, once again, became our escape and our refuge from the thicket of our parents' troubles. What had started out as a distressing event became an adventurous one. Wiley would disappear into the first rays of light and be gone past dark. Just when we would all start to worry, he would appear with a snake on the end of his stick. A little beyond the clearing and around the back of the house, my brother and I squatted for endless hours on the edge of a clear cold running creek, mesmerized in a world brimming with slimy green frogs and slithery black snakes. My toes squeezed into the soft mud, I let the baby mosquitoes feed upon my arms and legs as I lay in wait for frogs, tadpoles, and eggs. I put them into clean, one-gallon mayonnaise jars with holes punched in the caps, and they became my frog evolution project, for which I won second prize in the St. Clement Parish science fair.*

*From our porch, we looked out upon tall ripe towers of okra ready to be picked. Mother said she didn't know how to cook okra any way but boiled. Daddy insisted on variations each night for supper: okra casserole, okra gumbo, and even stuffed okra. Having the job of harvesting this abundant crop, Wiley and I hated the smell of it, but because my father was so proud of this vegetable's massive growth, we kept our mouths shut. "From seeds! From seeds!" he exclaimed, as my brother and I labored under a bushel load. Emerging from the little chicken coop directly behind our house each morning, he enthusiastically announced, "We have eggs!" I later learned that Daddy took our eggs to New Orleans and sold them to Norma.*

*To mark the beginning of my womanhood, Mama Lee was giving me a piece of white Samsonite luggage on each birthday. She cut out pictures for me from fashion magazines and we talked about what it would be like to live in Hawaii or California. I don't think she had ever been anywhere herself, but she encouraged me. I got the feeling that my grandmother saw the chance to live her life differently through me. I rebelled against many of her attempts to mold and shape me, believing that following her would mean abandoning my mother. My father had changed his tune about my seeing boys; at sixteen, I was allowed to go on dates Mama Lee arranged with the sons of her well-to-do clients, referring to them as appropriate young men. My grandmother decided that she wanted to adopt me and to arrange for my debut into Kemper society, which, in the 1950s, was every white girl's dream. My father put his foot down, saying, "No, absolutely and most definitely no." I rejected the idea, too — I had to stay with my family so I could keep close watch over my mother. For the nine months we lived "out in the sticks," I was a Cinderella wearing smart clothes and shoes that Mama Lee supplied, dating properly brought up boys whose names were on college fund accounts. Still, no matter where I went, who I dated, or what I wore, when I returned home it was to the web that held my family captive.*

*Mother was sick all through her pregnancy, and Big Mama, the woman who represented all goodness to me, was dying, although I didn't know it then. In my family nothing ever seemed to be known until the reality was upon us as if it had dropped from the sky without any warning. When we heard Big Mama's death rattles, we were stopped dead in our tracks as if struck dumb by the fact of her leaving. The grief of her death had hardly begun when Mother was rushed to the hospital to give birth to Davy. While Mother was gone I cleaned and cooked in her place, which gave my father a chance to laugh at my culinary creations. A couple of nights he cooked and, although he was a good cook, we would go hungry — he made pound cakes, ten of them, and mayonnaise, gallon jars of it. After supper one evening my father sat on the screened-in front porch, swatting flies, shucking oysters, and drinking, with a bottle sitting right out on the table, which I had never seen him do before. I pretended to be busy in the kitchen just so I wouldn't have to sit with him, but out of the corner of my eye I watched him. He seemed afraid; I felt he wanted us around just to help him feel better. It was rare for Mother to be away from home, and this was really the first time we had been alone with our father. It felt strange. We didn't know him. It was lonely without Mother's comforting presence.*

# DOUBLE RING CEREMONY

I was nine months pregnant when your father did finally get the marriage with Norma annulled. He made arrangements for us at a Methodist Church. We had a double ring ceremony! Your father placed a ring on my finger and I placed one on his finger. He kissed me like he really meant it — I couldn't believe this was really happening again and we were going to get our lives straightened out. J.W. acted like he was really truly happy. Of course, he acted like this every time we got married. I felt bad 'cause I was pregnant. The preacher's wife gave me a bouquet of roses and kissed me on the cheek.

As we were walking out that church door, I'll never forget what your daddy said to me. "Won't Norma be ready to kill us both when she finds out that we're married again? I wish there was some way she could find out — wouldn't she be mad!" I said, "What are you talking about her for — why would you bring her name up for!" He started laughing. "Now we're safe — nobody can hurt us now..." He put his arm around me and we went on down the road. We didn't tell nobody where we'd been. Our life just kept on going.

The day Davy was born me and J.W. had a fuss the night before. I had slept on the couch and I woke up at five o'clock in the morning and I was hemorrhaging. I managed to pull myself off the couch and I woke J.W. up. It didn't suppose to be time for the baby — the next thing I remember is seeing this big light over my head. I thought, something's wrong! I turned my head and there was my doctor looking at me. "You're hemorrhaging pretty bad and we can't get the baby in position for you to have a normal birth." J.W. was out in the hall pacing up and down and he was drinking. The doctor went out and told him. The baby wasn't born till eleven o'clock that night. I couldn't have him normal... they had to cut me open.

The next morning the doctor walked in and said he was sorry to tell me that your new little brother, Davy, had a broken leg. The doctor had to jerk him out so fast his leg got broken. They put a cast on his little leg and told me it would be about three to six weeks before they'd know.

When we took the baby back to the hospital on the third week I

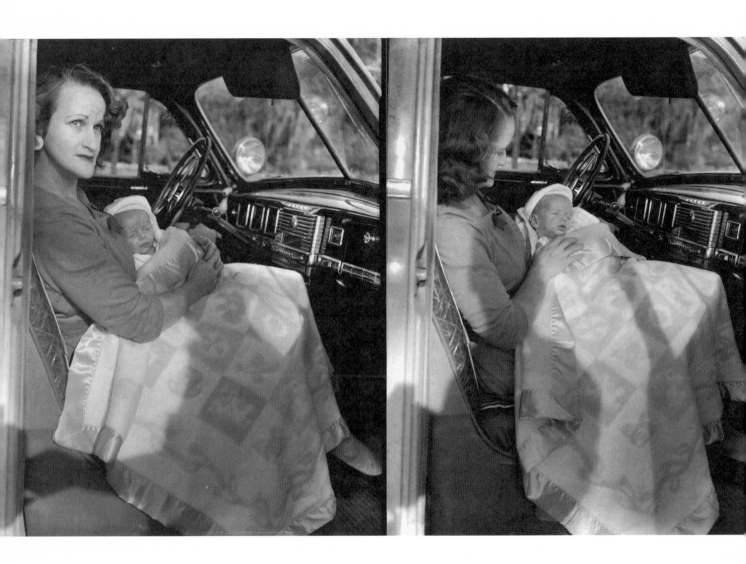

was a nervous wreck. The doctor came and J.W. had the baby in his arms and I wouldn't go in there where they were at all. I walked up and down the hall. I could hear him sawing that cast off his little leg. Well, I cried and prayed and I said, "Oh, dear God, please, please help that poor little baby. I've had so many problems. Please don't let this happen to him." A few minutes later the door opened and the doctor and your father walked out with Davy. I was standing in the middle of the hall crying. The doctor walked over to me and he said, "What are you crying for . . . everything is okay."

IN MY JUNIOR YEAR OF HIGH SCHOOL WE WERE BACK IN NEW ORLEANS, *living in a rambling two-story Greek Revival duplex. Across the street loomed St. Vincent DePaul mental hospital, where my father, in his growing need for more money to support his double life, got a job moonlighting as a night watchman. A .38 caliber special military police revolver and holster lay next to his bed. Our home had taken on an abandoned appearance, chairs and tables scratched and gouged from all the moving about, nothing matching anything else; wallpaper and curtain patterns collided, glass cracked across faces in picture frames, a shade that had once belonged on a huge lamp now swallowed up a much smaller replacement. Daddy made us join the Methodist Church and got it into his head that we should all be going together. Our forced Sunday outings to the Carrollton Avenue Methodist Church were a miserable effort on his part to do the right thing. We stood mumbling the words to songs we didn't know, pretending to be a family for an hour every week.*

*Every move we made, it was Mother who unpacked the boxes, put curtains on the windows and pictures on the walls. After our family left Kentucky, my mother never really kept house again. She tried, but her attempts were ghostly motions. It was as if her body remembered, but her mind could not tell her what needed to be swept most. One spot would get cleaner and cleaner, while a dirty corner went unnoticed. My mother continued to press scarlet color into her lips every morning, but her high heels gathered dust balls as they stood lined up against the wall opposite the bed she sometimes shared with my father.*

*I remembered the day I saw her use her hand as a dust pan. I was coming in from play but stopped outside the screen door and watched my mother, bent over a pile of dirt, place her hand parallel to it, and with one quick flick of the broom sweep it into her hand. The dirt lay there, still and dead, as if it were some kind of rare archeological remains. I ran back out to play, but the image remained in my mind.*

*My brother Wiley was more like Mother than I was; they both had sunny, caring dispositions. But during these days, my mother's smile was like sunlight being set free from its dark cloud cover, and, most of the time, her face was set in a frown. She didn't seem to care anymore. Her shoulders sloped downward as her waistline grew larger. She baked and ate layer cakes, cherry cobblers, sugar cookies, and lemon meringue pies. Her small frame became shapeless, the sleeves of her house-dresses squeezing so tightly that the flesh of her arms overflowed like warm rising* bread. When I began working, I bought my mother nice things to wear — lacy, silky bras, slips, and underwear. I wanted beautiful things to be next to her body, which had nurtured and protected me. She wouldn't wear them, saying they were too nice for her.

As part of my plan to free myself from the life my parents had spun, I got a job working on Saturdays at Lerner's, a small ladies' dry goods store on Canal Street. It was my first real job, and I tried hard to do well. "May I help you choose a skirt to go with that blouse?" "Oh, you look fantastic in that sweater—yellow is such a great color!" My coworkers, lifers on the job, were friendly at first but then began openly expressing a dislike for my style. "Slow down, honey, it's only one o'clock in the afternoon, we're gonna be here till five." I got fired for spending too much time with the customers. On my next job I spent all day lining up, sizing, and pricing panties, girdles, and brassieres at a five-and-dime store. I loved going into the employees' entrance, skipping up the back stairs above the glare of men loading garbage, proudly pulling out my card marked "Clarkson, P.," and punching in on the time clock — every minute meant money. I felt a new power. When my father found out where I was getting the money for all my new clothes, he very efficiently squashed my power by setting up a payment schedule for my room and board.

# SUNDAYS

Your father and I didn't have no relationship at all after your little brother Davy was two years old. We were just companions. He just lived there. I lived there. He went to work. He came back. I had meals on the table. He'd eat. I'd eat. Davy'd eat. After supper he'd go off till ten, ten thirty, come back and I'd be in bed and he would come in there and go to bed and go to sleep. He never would ask me did I want to go some place, even to the grocery store. I kept house and cooked and took care of Davy. He came and went when he wanted to. I wasn't very happy. He acted very unconcerned.

All the fussing that went on right then was 'cause your father never wanted to go anyplace with us. One week he told me, "I just don't like people. I have to put up with people down at the office. When I come home, I like to be free!" He never wanted you all to have friends. You could bring home a perfectly nice girl and when she left he would say, "Don't bring her here again . . . I don't like her looks."

On Sundays especially, I would ask him, "Why don't you drive us down to the park, J.W., Davy needs to go someplace." He'd say, "I'll take you all and I'll sit in the car while you do whatever you want to do." One Sunday he drove us to the park and I said, "Come on, J.W., why don't you get out of the car and play ball with Davy?" He wouldn't do it.

You kids were my strength. If I hadn't had my kids, I don't know what I'd done. I enjoyed you all. You all was my life, there wasn't nothin' else. Back in Kemper when Wiley was in the fifth grade, he was in a little play at school and I thought we should go. I went by myself and I was so proud of Wiley. Your father refused to go. The night you graduated from high school I told your father, "You are

LOUISE LOOKING AT J.W., AUDUBON PARK, NEW ORLEANS, C. 1960

LOUISE HIDING BEHIND DAVY, AUDUBON PARK, NEW ORLEANS C. 1960

going to go to your daughter's graduation, aren't you?" I guess you remember, your father did not come with us.

I could make it during the week someway or another, but Sunday was my lonesome day. I didn't have friends. I didn't have money. Davy and me sat out front on the porch steps like two dummies. We'd watch the cars with the families coming and going up and down the street. I wondered, "Why is it that everybody else has somebody and I don't have nobody?" I got so I didn't even want to sit on the front porch Sunday afternoons because I didn't want anybody to see me out there by myself.

I got so sick of not having any money I started searching his pockets at night or when he'd take a bath and I'd take a bill or two out of his wallet. I knew that was the only way I could get money out of him.

MY FATHER WAS A MAD JUGGLER. BY THE TIME I WAS SIXTEEN, HE WAS *living a double life, keeping both my mother and Norma suspended between marriage and divorce. Borrowing money from loan sharks, and with the help of alcohol and pills (pink for tension, white for sleeping, green for depression), my father juggled his two families and somehow managed to keep all his balls in the air. When Mother questioned his whereabouts, he crushed her, rising up and roaring like a sleeping giant angered at the audacity of a lower being. His favorite line was "I'm free, white and twenty-one — I can damn well do what I please!"*

*My father's daybooks, in which he recorded household finances, were lined up on the shelf in his home office. The moment we left Kentucky, he began compul-*

*sive record keeping in these books. He noted that when he was holding Louise's hand in the hospital at 7:30 A.M. on the day Davy was born, he drove a hundred miles to be in divorce court with Norma and her toddler at 10 A.M. These legal-sized books covered in faded gray cloth gave witness to what my father's life had become. He accounted for every penny spent: "on hand .10, Colored beggar .05, dog food .34, whiskey 1.40, coffee .15, 1.00 in cuff link box, car fare .20, parking .05" and so on. He also listed routine matters: "washed socks this morning," "had Chevrolet greased," "Roving Heels put on my Florsheim shoes." Interspersed with these were events of more emotional import, such as "Norma pregnant," "L & I looked at house and got M today," "L & I had a violent argument today about bills — she hit me with shoes and threw 2 chairs — I slapped her on top of head," as well as the logging in of his wife's menstrual periods and when he had intercourse with one or another of the two women: "Had IC with N at 4:00 P.M. this afternoon." There were notes on historical events — "Hurricane 'Carla' building up in Yucatan Peninsula & headed towards La-Tex coast," "stock market fell heavy today" — and inventories of medications, furniture, clothes, and books. Mother's Day gifts, to both women and the two mothers-in-law, were noted.*

*My father's needs permeated the air we breathed, spilling into every crevice and corner. Sometimes when I arrived home from school loaded down with books and homework and full of stories to tell, the house would be a mess. Mother hadn't washed the breakfast dishes; dirty coffee cups and ashtrays filled with cigarette butts littered the rooms. The smell of burnt coffee ate up the fresh air. Daddy hadn't gone to work, and the shades were still drawn. Davy, age three, would be sitting in his little rocking chair, rocking. My mother would attempt some sort of explanation barely audible under the chatter of an overburdened air conditioner. "J.W., the kids are home from school, let me go and get this house cleaned up!" Mother pleaded. "Patricia, your mother and I don't see eye to eye on things," he would add. Mother's chair was warm from her sitting in it all day, listening to J.W.'s troubles. Daddy didn't question Mother as he once had; now he used her as a way to discharge all his emotional needs. As I headed for the kitchen to begin supper as I was told to do, grumbling under my breath, my father stood up to slap me. "Don't sass me, young lady!"*

## A PRISONER

You and your daddy had started arguing so much, you moved out and went to live with your girlfriend's family. I said, "Oh, Patricia, please don't go, please don't leave..." You said, "I'm sorry, Mother, but I have to go." One time after you moved out, you came to visit me. "Mother, go get your pocketbook, I'm gonna take you shopping."

"I don't have a pocketbook."

"Okay, I'll give you my pocketbook!"

"Well, what am I supposed to put in it . . . I don't have anything to put in it."

You went in there and found a compact and a lipstick. I remember I felt so clumsy carrying a pocketbook 'cause I wasn't used to it. You fixed my hair. When we got down to Canal Street, I was on pins and needles for you to hurry and get me home. I was afraid of your father just like I was when you were a little girl. Nothing had changed.

I guess the end really came for me when one day your father came in and told me, "You know, Louise, we shouldn't be living over here in New Orleans. My mother needs us back over near her in Kemper." His mother had been sick about a year already with bone cancer. A few days later he went back in the darkroom and stayed and stayed. I thought he was working on pictures. When he came out, he opened the door and said, "Well, I've got all my boxes packed up." I kept telling him I didn't want to go! He wouldn't listen to me! He forced me into doing something again that I didn't want to do! He didn't come in and talk to me and ask me what I thought about it. No! He made all the decisions and then came in and told me that we were gonna do it! I had this terrible feeling that your father wasn't coming with us. Nobody don't know what I went through . . . that night before and all that day I was very emotional. I was crying all the time I was putting things in boxes. I was a child at heart. I wasn't grown up. He had me so brainwashed I couldn't think for myself. I tried to think of some way out . . . but I couldn't think! Who could I turn to! My mother was never someone I could go to with my troubles. I didn't want to try asking her for help now. Your father took advantage of me because I was kind. Norma was mean and he was scared of her. J.W. didn't want me as a wife, but as a mother.

I remember the last night at the house, looking at that little green light flickering on his recorder [Dictaphone], tears came in my eyes 'cause I knew it was all over. Your father told me he would get a room and he would see me later. I thought, "This is the end. It's all over." I felt very sad.

He moved us back over to Kemper, me and Davy and Wiley. The house was small and so dark and dingy that we had to burn lights in the daytime. I was so unhappy I couldn't undo the boxes and try to make a home and fix the house up. All I did really was fix the beds and unpack some dishes. The house was a wreck.

Wiley was never the same again. J. W. had pulled him out of school in New Orleans — Wiley told me he didn't want to be around his daddy. Every time J. W. would come around Wiley would run away. I couldn't make him go to school. One of his teachers sent us a note saying they wanted to see us. Jackie Lee knew this and she told J. W. One morning J. W. showed up at the house, came in and tore the pants right off of Wiley and spanked him . . . beat him with a belt. I felt so sorry for Wiley . . . he ran off. He got into trouble with the police. He stayed out all night. I was worried to death all the time. I was there alone with these two kids . . . a teenager and a four-year-old! Davy didn't go to kindergarten; his daddy wouldn't send him. He failed first grade. The teacher said he didn't even know how to catch a ball. He didn't know how to hold his hands out. The ball would come to him and it would hit his stomach and just roll down. I got out there in the yard and tried to play ball with him after I heard that.

Just like I thought, your father never did come and move in with us. He would come and spend the weekends but that didn't do no good. He said he had to live in New Orleans for business reasons. When he brought me over there and put me in that terrible-looking house I felt like he'd buried me. Our life just was no life at all! I got so I just didn't care. All I wanted to do was just sit. I was scared because I realized I couldn't think for myself. It seemed like he had

LOUISE, AGE FORTY-THREE, C. 1961–62

me hypnotized — he had me programmed. He'd say "yes" and I'd say "yes." He'd say "no" and I'd say "no." I was scared because I knew I was a prisoner.

J.W. would come in on Friday nights with big smiles and jokes and he'd bring groceries. On the third week he said, "Are you feeling any better?"

"No, I'm not!"

"Louise, why don't you try to get up and do something around this house?"

I said, "What's the use? I don't like it here. I'm lonely. I don't go no place. I don't have any friends. I don't have nothing to live for."

"Well, why don't you go over to see Mother?"

"I do go over there and see her but when I come back it's the same old thing over here."

So I stayed unhappy and depressed. On the fourth week, when your daddy came over there and could see how bad off I was, he moved us out of that awful house in Kemper and found us a duplex back in New Orleans. I kept asking, "J.W., why is it you have not moved back with us?" He just said, "Oh, I will later." Patricia, I knew he was with her but I had given up trying to bring him back.

I really think sometimes that the reason I never could fight your father was because of the way I was raised. My mother bossed me and told me I couldn't do nothing. I never would talk back. I would always do exactly what she told me to because if I didn't do it she would punish me. If I did anything that my mother didn't like she would put me inside of a closet on a chair and make me sit there. One day I sat and sat there. Finally I said, "Mama, I'm getting very hungry, can I please come out?" She said, "Oh, Louise, I forgot I left you in there!" I was a little bitty kid. I had been in there all day. I don't even remember what I had done. One time she told me, "I had you to work for me." She started laughing but she really meant it. I believed it, 'cause when I was a child, I cleaned house and I nursed my mother the whole time.

My father was such a kind man. I got up many a morning and he would be sitting in the kitchen talking to some stranger. I'd ask Mama, "Who's that in the kitchen?" "No telling!" Later on I would hear my daddy say, "Now, have you had enough breakfast?" My daddy would fix a bag lunch and give it to this hobo before he left. It got so that we had hobos knocking on our door. When my daddy wasn't there my mother would lock the doors and we couldn't let anybody in. That's how Mama was . . . Mama was for Mama! I'm more like my father than my mother. No, I'm not like Mama at all! If I'd been more like her, maybe your father wouldn't have treated me like he did. You got to be hard sometimes, too. You can't be kind all the time. When I married your father, he said, "All the things that your mother makes you do you'll never have to do, you can do whatever you want to do." But, after I married, I felt like it was the same way. I was told what to do, where to go and I never had no money of my own. I was afraid of my mother and I was afraid of my husband. It seemed like to me I married a man that was just like my mother. I feel like I was never free. In my life I was never free.

I look back on my life and I don't know why or how in the world I ever put up with the things I did. Lord, I wish I had my life to live all over again, things would have been different for me. I would have seen to it that I got me a good education and learned to be a good nurse. I didn't think I could make it on my own. I thought I could never go out and face the world. I never had nobody to ever stand behind me and encourage me. If a girl doesn't have a trade and doesn't know how to take care of herself, she'll be in some *low land*. She'll be lost. She won't know what to do. She won't know where to go. I tell you, every girl should know how to do something. I wouldn't advise any girl to ever get married unless they have a job and know something before, because you never know when you will need it.

MY FATHER'S PRACTICE OF RECORDING THE MUNDANE INCREASED. NOW, *however, instead of using my mother as his subject (where she went, what she wore, who she spoke to, when she washed the clothes), he focused on my little brother's bodily functions: sleep (time and length), weight (with shoes, without shoes — A.M., P.M.), food intake (time of consumption, description, quantity, quality), appearance (pallor, color, eyes), energy (tired, active), and bowel movements (frequency, time, size). Mother had her hands full providing Daddy with the data on Davy. Daddy gave Davy daily enemas, hand fed him, and kept him home in bed, nursing his real or imaginary colds, constipation, anemia, and poor appetite. Mother was blamed for Davy's watery eyes, paleness, loss of appetite, crankiness — anything. At first she would try to defend herself and then would say, "I guess I shouldn't have let him go out, I won't do it again, I didn't think it would hurt, I guess I did wrong." It was a game they played; Mother said what Daddy wanted to hear just so he would leave her alone. I only wish Mother could have said, "NO! I AM NOT TO BLAME! GO TO HELL!" Then the game might have been over.*

*I thought it odd for a child to have this sort of record as part of his growing up*

DADDY WAS MYSTERIOUS. HE DRANK STRAIGHT VODKA. THERE WAS A BOTTLE IN THE PANTRY. I CAN'T HARDLY REMEMBER HIM SPENDING THE NIGHT AT THE HOUSE. I THOUGHT THAT'S THE WAY IT WAS. MOTHER'D ALWAYS SAY HE WAS ON THE ROAD. SOMETIME HE'D SPANK ME, BUT I GOT THE FEELING HE FELT SORRY FOR ME AND DIDN'T WANT TO SPANK ME. HE SMOKED BACK THEN AND HE'D LAY ON THE COUCH WITH ME AND WATCH TELEVISION. MY ROOM WAS A SICK BAY. DADDY HAD MADE A TENT OVER THE BED AND PUT A VAPORIZER THERE FILLED WITH SOME MEDICINE AND I WAS SUPPOSED TO LAY THERE BREATHING IT. EVERYTHING HAD TO BE PERFECT. HE WOULD COME AT LUNCH TIME AND FEED ME. HE WROTE DOWN WHAT I ATE IN A BOOK. I COULDN'T EVER GO TO SCHOOL. HE KEPT ME HOME SO MUCH I FAILED THE FIRST GRADE.—DAVY

< DAVY, AGE FIVE, NEW ORLEANS, C. 1963

DADDY WAS ALWAYS LIKE A BUSINESSMAN, DRESSED UP AND READY TO GO OUT ALL THE TIME. I DON'T REMEMBER US EVER GOING ANYWHERE TOGETHER. HE HAD A WAY OF MAKING YOU FEEL SYMPATHETIC TOWARDS HIM. HE LOOKED LIKE HE WAS HELPLESS AND YOU JUST HAD TO GIVE HIM SOME HELP. MOM WAS THE LITTLE NUN WHO WORKED AROUND THE HOUSE. HE NEVER SAID MUCH TO ME. I FELT LIKE A MISFIT—I DIDN'T FEEL LIKE I BLENDED IN WITH ANYTHING OR ANYBODY. I USED TO HAVE THIS RECURRING DREAM, IT WAS LIKE A DAY-DREAM OR DAYMARE—IT WOULD HAPPEN WHEN I WOULD CLOSE MY EYES, A ROARING SOUND, LIKE A BIG GIANT WHEEL ROLLING. THIS HAPPENED FOR A LONG TIME—IT USED TO BOTHER ME A LOT—I REMEMBER I WOULD PUT MY HANDS OVER MY EARS 'CAUSE I COULD HEAR THE NOISE. I COULD ACTUALLY HEAR THE NOISE OF THESE WHEELS ROLLING. I WOULD GO LAY IN MY BED AND PUT MY HANDS OVER MY EARS AND SQUEEZE REAL HARD, TO TRY TO GET THE NOISE TO QUIT.—WILEY

< WILEY, AGE FIFTEEN, NEW ORLEANS, C. 1961–63

rather than the usual one of birthday parties and family picnics. Davy hardly looked up or spoke. One morning when he was nearly three years old, I stood at the window watching him at play in the backyard. He was digging in the dirt next to the fence between our house and the neighbors'. Sammy, a kid about Davy's age, was working on a similar hole adjacent to Davy's on the other side of the fence. The two kids began conversing, probably something like "This is a big hole, ain't it?" When Sammy's mother looked out her kitchen window and saw her son talking to Davy, she came galloping out and grabbed her beloved child away from the boy with the raging father. The neighbor's little boy was scolded and warned not to talk to "that Clarkson" boy. The next time Davy said "Hi" to his neighbor, Sammy ran off.

WILEY WAS DRIFTING AWAY. WHEN DADDY WAS HOME, HE TOOK OUT much of his emotional frustration on Wiley. "Leave me alone. I don't have time. Can't you see I'm busy!" This was a typical response when John Wiley III, the spitting image of his father, would dare ask a question, usually nothing more than "Daddy, can I borrow your flashlight?"

As a girl I was protected and looked after, regardless of my father's motives, but Wiley did not receive the same care. Whatever house we lived in, I was always given a room of my own, but Wiley had to sleep on couches, in hallways, or on *porches. Maybe Daddy thought a boy was tougher, but my brother was a gentle, kind, naive boy.*

*When he was enrolled in Sophie B. Wright, Wiley began traveling with a rough bunch of kids, choosing friends from shattered families, usually those without a father. Ultimately he would quit school before he finished the eighth grade. Mother felt sorry for us kids, so she was a pushover. Many times when Wiley didn't come home all night, Daddy would go out looking for him; often when I left my after-school job, I would find my father waiting for me outside in his company car. He and I would go scout the Irish Channel neighborhoods around Magazine Street, where Wiley hung out, until we found him. The next day he would be gone again. My father was oddly supportive whenever Wiley or I got into trouble, acting like a big lawyer pleading a case. But by the time he tried to help Wiley by meeting with school counselors, truant officers, and law officials, it was too late.*

*One night when he was fifteen, my brother was walking along a commercial strip on Magazine Street. He saw a man drive slowly by with his window down, his free hand draped over the front seat. The man stopped and motioned for Wiley to come over to the open window of his Mercury. Wiley knew what he wanted. He knew other boys who made money like this. He got into the strange man's car. That night my brother experienced sex for the first time. His friends called this activity "rolling fruits."*

THE CATHOLIC CHURCH GAVE ME SPIRITUAL REFUGE FROM MY UNRAVEL-
ing family. Without my father's consent, I secretly converted to Catholicism. When
I walked into the sanctuary of flickering light, myrrh and frankincense, smiling
plaster saints, Jesus and Latin, I felt safe and cleansed. Every Wednesday
evening for six months I faithfully went to the office of Father Ryan at St.
Stephen's for my catechism lesson. He smoked cigars and drank wine while I
recited what I had set to memory. Before I left, he blessed me with holy water, and
I ran home in the dark cool air feeling that I had found a place where I could be
happy.

Every chance I got I made the sign of the cross; my finger, damp with imagined
holy water, would go to the middle of my forehead, then directly to my heart, then
gently up to my left shoulder and over just as gently to the right. "In the name of
the Father and the Son and the Holy Spirit. Amen," I would say silently, feeling
that my troubles would be magically lifted.

High school life was smoother for me than it might have been because of my boyfriend, Johnny, who was a funny, easygoing guy from a working-class Irish family.
With Johnny's love, the Catholic Church, and my job, I stayed afloat. I picked
friends from good families and stuck it out in high school. Many of my girlfriends
had to drop out because they were pregnant. Johnny and I came dangerously
close but never went all the way; we were saving up for our wedding night. It was
actually my father's warning that kept me in school. He lectured me nonstop: "You
won't get anywhere in this world without an education!" His career advice was

*that I should become a secretary. "It's an easy job for a woman," he said. His sec-*
*retary had it made, he told me; she took long lunches and several breaks a day*
*and got a good salary. I didn't know anyone who went to college, so, in my senior*
*year of high school, I decided I would take my father's advice. I worked half a*
*school day in the New Orleans office of Metro-Goldwyn-Mayer and in the after-*
*noons attended classes in typing, stenography, and business math.*

*A few months before graduation day I left home for the second time, after another*
*explosion with my father. One Saturday when I had a picnic planned with some*
*friends, my little brother began crying for a piece of the watermelon that sat cooling*
*in the refrigerator. Mother said, "No, that's for your sister's picnic." Davy kept*
*whining until Daddy began demanding that I cut it open. I refused. He and I*
*began wrestling with the five-pound melon as if it were a matter of life or death.*
*Mother tried to separate us. Davy was crying, "Daddy, don't hurt Sissy...please,*
*Daddy, it's okay, I don't want any...water...melon." (Remembering Davy's voice,*
*I am filled with remorse at my simultaneous neediness and selfishness. In many*
*ways I was like my father — anger boiled up inside of me and spilled out onto*
*whoever was around. If I sensed discrimination or abuse of any kind from my*
*boyfriend, Johnny, I tore into him with gale force.) The melon slipped from our*
*hold and crashed onto the kitchen floor. For a moment we all stood silently look-*
*ing down at the pink frothy watermelon guts. Then I fled in bare feet and ran to*
*a phone to call Johnny; the next day he helped me move to a girlfriend's house.*

*The few months left of my senior year were spent in the embrace of my friend's family. My father did not come to watch me graduate. I didn't expect him to. He was in a dark, dark place. My mother sat alone, all smiles and hugs for her daughter.*

*Six months after Johnny and I graduated in our powder-blue caps and gowns, I dismissed all our plans for marriage and quite casually broke up with him. I began dating Evan, a psychology student at Tulane University. We were quite a picture together. He was a doctor's son from a small town in New York, a preppy wearing loafers with white socks. I was a working girl with a beehive hairdo, eyeliner, and foundation. I never knew why Evan pursued me. I loved him as I loved my father, with faltering suspicion. I didn't believe he could possibly care about me, so I pretended not to care about him. He was important to me not as a boyfriend but as my first guide to a world far from the one I knew.*

*On my own, I shaped a life without my family. I was determined not to be like my mother. I wanted to be free, to come and go as I pleased, and to have cash in my pockets. I saved my money and bought an old black Ford that had to be started without a key — the owner told me he had lost it. I taught myself how to drive late at night on the straight road along the lake front, where I practiced turns and parking. At eighteen I was still too young for a Louisiana driver's license without parental approval, which my father refused, so for three years I drove illegally.*

*Dressing in spiked heels and matching pocketbook, each morning I marched through the French Quarter, where I now lived, to my new secretarial job. After work I sat in bars reading existentialist writers and fending off interested male patrons. I enrolled in a night class in anthropology at Tulane University. My friends from New York enjoyed making fun of my dialect and misuse of the English language. I tried hard to correct myself, appreciating the help however unkind some of the criticism seemed. At lunch time I went to the New Orleans Public Library and came back to the office loaded down with books. My great goal was to improve myself.*

*During this time I didn't see my family much; I was living in a kind of self-protective state, floating above the growing chaos that was enveloping my mother and brothers. Sometimes on Friday evenings I'd go home to have supper. "How are you, Mother?" I would inquire. She'd smile and say, "Just fine, just fine..." I knew she wasn't "fine," but I was selfishly happy in my new life and inquired no further.*

*Two years after I graduated from high school, I packed my white Samsonite luggage. I was going to travel. My father came to talk me out of it, sending Mother to my apartment door. "Patricia, your father's downstairs, please come down and talk to him." My mother's eyes were full of love for me. I rolled my eyes at her, remembering my first date with Johnny, when my father sent her into the movie theater to be sure the boy hadn't eaten me alive. Fortifying myself, I walked down the stairs, recalling how Mother laughed about Daddy's agility with words, his salesmanship.*

*I sat in the front seat opposite the giant man I was defying, while he tried to convince me not to leave on my journey. I felt strong and determined. How could I trust his advice? I felt he was just trying to control me. My mother sat in the back seat not saying a word, but I knew how she felt; she supported me and wished she had my guts. "Patricia, the grass isn't any greener on the other side...I've been there...a rolling stone gathers no moss...," he said, looking concerned and sad. (My father's suffering failed to touch me as a young girl, but, later in my adult life, I would find myself struck down by memory whenever I saw a leaning, round-shouldered, tall man. I would sometimes even follow such a man, as if by so doing I could reunite with my father.) It was a poignant moment as we sat there that day on the corner of St. Louis and Chartres, the old guard attempting to pass on bits and pieces of wisdom he himself had failed to heed. This was to be the last time I would see my father. I didn't think about such a possibility then; I was anxious to get on with my life. I opened the car door and stepped out. "Bye, Daddy," I said. Looking into my father's eyes at that moment, I knew I loved him, and every hug I would give a man thereafter would be the hug I didn't give my father that day.*

*On his 1950 income tax form, my father listed his occupation as "salesman"; my mother's was "housewife." On the 1040 form in 1966, his occupation was "insurance adjuster"; my mother's was "none." Social security number: none.*

*The final chapter of J.W. and Louise's marriage tale took place in Texas. Norma nagged my father to take a job that paid more money and to move to a state where common-law marriage was legal. He begged my mother on his knees until she promised to go with him. "I've got a good job waiting. It all depends on you, Louise. You have to help me! It'll be great. Texas is a big country, big enough for all of us. Promise me you'll go!" Everything was sold. J.W. promised to buy Louise all new appliances and furnishings for "a new start," he said. "This will be our chance." Wiley refused to go. Daddy, Mother, and Davy were all travel-ing west with their belongings pulled behind in a trailer. Wiley was camped out in the shell of what had been their home in New Orleans. Mother remembers that Daddy cried as they drove away, leaving Wiley behind.*

*Thirty years later as I sit here thinking of my seventeen-year-old brother left penniless and homeless in New Orleans, I want to reach back, take him in my arms, and carry him to safety. But I was battling my own demons when my family left for Texas; I had learned that I was pregnant.*

## "LOVE, DADDY"

When your daddy brought us to Texas, I felt like I was in another country. If I had had wings, I'd have put them on and flown back to New Orleans. Your father was like somebody that I didn't even know. He acted like he was going out of his mind—he talked to me about his insurance policies in case anything happened to him. He never moved in with us. Davy was just seven years old. "Mama, where's Daddy going?" "He's just going to work, Davy." I had to lie to him. To get the money for our bills, I would have to go on a bus and take Davy to a drugstore thirty minutes away. J.W. would meet us there. Sometimes I could see little tears coming out of the corner of his eyes. He would slip me a plain white envelope with the money inside. On the outside of the envelope he would always write "Love, Daddy." On the way home one day after meeting his father, Davy said, "Mother, you know what I wish, I wish Daddy would come in and put his shoes underneath our bed like he used to do." By then, Davy was eleven. When he said that to me, it felt like a slice was cut right out of my heart.

Sometimes I would see J.W. passing in front of our house. He'd pass but he would never stop. He had become a ghost in my life. The feeling had already gone. Early on in our marriage I think if he'd absolutely gone off and left me completely and said goodbye forever I would of died. That's the truth, but now my love for him had died—I didn't have no feeling towards him at all. I don't know how he felt towards me. I didn't feel he was my husband—he was a stranger.

Then after a while your father told me it was too risky us meeting him and from now on he could only send me the money—that's all he give me, was the rent money. I had to go down and try to get food stamps. It was awful. I have never been so desperate in all my life. It wasn't long before your father called and said, "I just don't have the money no more, I'm having a hard time myself." I was so upset and worried I had to call my mother and ask her to come and help me. Wiley came, too, and tried to be a father to Davy, but it didn't work out. Wiley was just too hard on Davy. Of course, that's what he learned from his daddy.

WHEN WILEY CAME TO TEXAS TO HELP MOTHER, I REMEMBER IT WAS NIGHT-TIME — IT WAS DARK. HE CAME TO THE DOOR. HE WAS HUGE. HE WAS A BIG MAN, AND REAL MUSCULAR. I SAID, "WHO ARE YOU...WHAT DO YOU WANT?" HE SAID, "I'M YOUR BROTHER!" I DIDN'T RECOGNIZE HIM. I REBELLED AGAINST WILEY. I DIDN'T WANT HIM TO BE MY DAD. I WAS BITTER 'CAUSE DADDY COULDN'T BE MY DAD. WILEY WAS REAL DOMINATING TOWARD ME, PATRICIA. HE USED TO THREATEN ME. "I'M GOING TO GET YOU UP AND YOU'RE GOING DOWN TO GET A HAIRCUT, TODAY!" HE HAD A REAL BAD TEMPER — HE WOULD GET SO MAD, HE'D TURN RED. HE LOOKED LIKE THE DAMN "HULK" — HIS VEINS WOULD BE POPPING OUT — HE'D START SCREAMING TO THE TOP OF HIS — I THOUGHT THE WORLD WAS GONNA COME TO AN END. I THINK IT WAS WRONG HIM TRYING TO PLAY A DAD ROLE. PATRICIA, I USED TO HIDE IN THE CLOSETS FROM HIM. I WAS AFRAID WE'D GET INTO IT. IT WAS ABUSE IN WORDS. HE'D GET SO MAD, HE'D KNOCK DOWN DOORS. HE HAD A VOICE YOU COULD HEAR A MILE AWAY. HE TOOK OVER, HE WAS LIKE THE HUSBAND AND THE DADDY AND EVERYTHING. — DAVY

< WILEY ON THE DAY HE ARRIVED IN TEXAS, C. 1968

# "I'M NOT DEAD YET!"

I remember the last time I saw your father—it was early one morning. It was still dark outside. I was sound asleep and I heard a knock on the door. I got up and looked out and I didn't see no car.

I said, "Where's your car, J.W.?"

He said, "I parked it down about two or three blocks away."

"Why did you do that?"

"If they follow me I'm afraid she might make me lose my job . . . I don't trust her," he said. "I can't come back no more."

It was Davy's birthday. He was thirteen years old. J.W. had brought him a pair of cowboy boots. He said, "I want to go in there and lay them down beside Davy's bed and I'm going to put a little money there so he'll know I was here." He went in there and kissed Davy, and he laid those boots beside his bed and put some money in his hand.

He came back and looked around and he said, "Are you all getting along all right?"

I said, "Just fine." I looked up at him . . . his hair was so white and he looked so old, I felt sorry for him, he was such a lonesome, miserable man. When he started out the door, I said to him, "J.W., why don't you just go ahead and marry this woman and settle down and be a human being? Why are you living the life you're living? It's time, J.W.!" I remember he looked at me and he said, "I'm not dead yet . . . but you wanna kill me! Just leave things like they are . . . you never know, I might be back over here before you know it." He leaned over and kissed me and he just went out the door and I didn't see him no more.

When Davy got up, he said, "Daddy's been here."

I said, "Yes, he has."

HOME, GREENFIELD, KENTUCKY, 1989

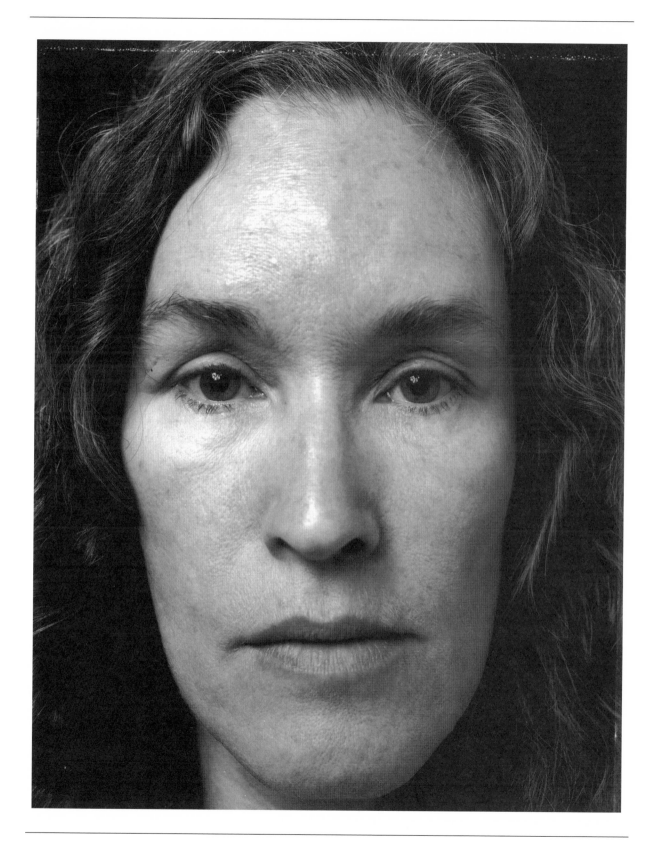

PATRICIA, SELF-PORTRAIT, NEW YORK, 1991

## EPILOGUE

*Twelve years later, it was a box of my father's pictures that precipitated Louise and J.W.'s final divorce. Davy found them. He told me that some of the pictures were of women, model types, and some of Daddy, nude and grinning in front of his old Chevy. One of Mother in a sexually suggestive pose so disgusted him that he burnt them all to ashes in the kitchen sink. It was Davy who pushed Mother to get a divorce from her husband, who had essentially become a bigamist.*

*J.W. became a phantom in our minds. We never saw him again, although we know he lives with Norma just a five-minute expressway ride from the home of Davy and his family. The younger of my brothers quit school at fifteen; by eighteen he was married, and by twenty he was a father. Davy was against having children, because, he said, "Something's wrong in our family. I don't want to pass that on to them." Today he has three children, ages sixteen, twelve, and seven, and works at three backbreaking jobs to provide a good home for them. He did manage to marry a nice girl and start a family, a feat that eluded Wiley and me for most of our lives, but he suffers mood swings, and worries that he will become like his father — "somebody weird," as he says.*

*My brother Wiley says love has left him with five black holes in his body. He has recently married for the sixth time. He has no children of his own. He says he wishes he were a woman because women have children, men have only work. In between his marriages, he has lived with Mother. He has read all the books and can give lectures on the subject of marriage and love. He remains good looking, kind and generous, and searches for a place to call home and a happy family to share it with.*

*After J.W. disappeared, Louise at age fifty-three applied for her very first social security number. When she began working at a day care center, she said, she felt like a "bird out of a cage." She opened a bank account and talked and giggled on the phone for as long as she wanted. With the help of newly acquired friends, she moved to a nicer house, and even bought a red dress. My mother appeared to be free of the constraints that had bound her for the thirty–three years of her marriage, but there are no miracles to report here. The truth is that Louise could never truly recover from all the years of deprivation. However, telling her stories had been cathartic, and now, when I ask for a story, she says she can't remember any.*

*Nearing the end of my childbearing years, I searched for the daughter whom I had placed for adoption in 1965. When I found Sonya, she had been renamed Jenny, and was a beautiful young woman who stood over me a full two heads in height. Last June on my wedding day, I held Jenny's arm as she gave me away in a torrent of wind and rain, lilacs and roses. I have married a good man, who is caring and gentle, who listens, and with whom I have created a partnership. In my closet I still have the briefcase of the first man I married, an alcoholic who drank himself to death. I can't seem to throw it away. I tried to bury it last year, but gave up when I discovered how hard it was to dig a hole big enough for a briefcase.*

# ACKNOWLEDGMENTS

The making of this book has been closely aligned with my life's journey. My sincere gratitude to all those who inspired, guided, supported, and believed in me during the many long years that it took to bring this work to conclusion. Thanks to my editor, JoAnne Prichard, for her courage in taking this book on and for her steady piloting of it. My appreciation to the superb staff at the University Press of Mississippi, especially to Carol Cox for her sensitive copyediting and to John Langston for his dedicated work on the excellent layout and design. My thanks to the organizations who have provided financial support: The National Endowment for the Arts, New York Foundation for the Arts, The MacDowell Colony, W. Eugene Smith Foundation, and the Kean College Grants office. I am especially thankful to Jane Peterson and Beatrix Gates for editing assistance; Zoya Gorelik for her invaluable photography assistance; Jim Rust of the Visual Artists Legal Defense Fund and attorney Ira Lowe for legal counsel; Bob Giard, Julia Skully, Marvin Heiferman, Germaine Clair, Jay Judge, Anne Marie Rousseau, Jill Korostoff of JAK DESIGN, and Anna Winand of ICP for helpful recommendations and the generous sharing of knowledge; Joyce Neimanas, whose enthusiasm for this project pushed me on from the beginning; Dr. Ruth Waelsch for a quiet place to write; my cousins Chuck and Camille and John and Kay for their important contribution to my knowledge of family history; Rosanne, Lucille, and Carole Honea-Muscari, valued old friends, who enlarged and sparked my memory. A heartfelt thanks to steadfast friends who gave of their precious time, encouraged, and offered advice of all kinds: Abby Heyman, David Heath, Carole Gallagher, Mary Kalergis, the late great writer Jane Howard, and longtime friend Via Wynroth. Most of all, I acknowledge with love and gratitude my mother and my brothers for their willingness to share their memories and stories; my daughter, Jenny, for her sweet and constant encouragement; and my husband, Larry, for his love and unwavering support.

*Library of Congress Cataloging-in-Publication Data*

Blue, Patt
    Living on a dream : a marriage tale / Patt Blue.
          p.      cm.
    ISBN 1-57806-057-5 (cloth) : alk. paper)
     1. Problem families—United States.  2. Family violence—
United States.  3. Abused wives—United States.  I. Title.
HV699.B563  1998
362.82'0973—dc21

                                  97-39452
                                      CIP